Every young adult needs *Adulting 101*. While Josh and Pete's first book taught readers what an adult does, this book shows readers who an adult is. *Adulting 101* teaches you how to fail well, develop grit, cultivate wisdom, manage conflict, and most importantly how to know yourself and others. Become who you were meant to be and give the gift of personal growth with this book.

—Bob Goff, Author of New York Times Best Sellers *Love Does*, *Everybody Always*, and *Dream Big*

If you're a twenty-something, or if you have a twenty-something in your life, this is the book for you. With their signature honesty and entertaining storytelling, Burnette and Hardesty show how to take the journey into adulthood with maturity, confidence, and boldness.

—Daniel H. Pink, Author of New York Times Best Sellers *When* and *Drive*

Everything you need to know for less stress and more success in the real world is right here. You don't have to figure it all out yourself. *Adulting 101* is your road map.

—Valorie Burton, CEO of The Coaching and Positive Psychology Institute and Author of national Best Seller *Successful Women Think Differently*

Adulting 101 Book 2 is one of the most helpful guides to growing up that you'll find. This book will transform your understanding of yourself, others, and the world around you in order to become a healthy, fulfilled adult. With their funny stories and profound truths, Josh and Pete provide a compass for twenty-somethings to navigate their inner life. This is the roadmap you've been looking for and one you will return to again and again.

—Mark Batterson, Author of New York Times Best Seller *The Circle Maker*

Self-examination can be a painful gift. It can create clarity of focus and appetite for change that normally doesn't exist, but it takes courage to go there. Pete and Josh show you how.

—Kristen Cavallo, CEO of The Martin Agency

This powerful book is a must-read for anyone in their twenties. The transition to the "real world" can be lonely as young adults step into a world of new responsibilities, expectations, and choices. Thankfully, Josh and Pete make the perfect guides for this time of life, and their book empowers readers to craft lives of meaning and fulfillment. Read it and feel a little more seen, a little less lonely, and a lot more prepared for the challenges ahead.

—Dr. Gordon Gee, President of West Virginia University

Adulting 101 Book 2 is a necessary, profound book for any young person trying to figure out adulthood. Becoming an adult brings many challenges, but Pete and Josh offer insight, wisdom, and practical advice that will launch young people into a greater future.

—Lavaedeay Lee, All-American Quarterback, author of *Position over Purpose*

An important guide for twenty-somethings on growing up and becoming confident, emotionally healthy individuals.

—Holley Gerth, Life Coach, Counselor, and Bestselling Author of *The Powerful Purpose of Introverts*

Adulting 101 Book 1 was an important guide for all of us who work with college students as we help them find their way. *Adulting 101 Book 2* takes it to another level with Pete and Josh's insights, wit, and deep understanding of the path to adulthood. I can't wait for colleagues, students, and young adults around the world to benefit from this great work. If you want to experience growth, this book is for you!

—Dr. Tim Miller, Vice President for Student Affairs, James Madison University

The more I dove into Adulting 101 Book 2, the longer the list became of young people, parents, and leaders who I want to read this book. By merging deep truth with relatable stories and practical ideas, Josh Burnette and Pete Hardesty offer a priceless guide to help you learn, live, and love better both now and for years to come.

—Kara Powell, PhD, Chief of Leadership Formation at Fuller Seminary and Executive Director of the Fuller Youth Institute

I've watched thousands of young adults make life-altering decisions in their transition to adulthood. This awesome book helps readers gain direction in decision-making and gives helpful footholds in applying wisdom to these situations. Get the upper hand on adulting by reading and applying this book.

—Jonathan Pokluda, Pastor and Author of *Welcome To Adulting* and *Outdated*

Institutions of higher learning will only be effective if they relentlessly pursue whole person education. To grow intellectually, emotionally, and spiritually is to grow into an adult of consequence. I've learned this happens only with daily intentionality, and that's where this book is valuable. Josh and Pete challenge with the right questions, identify the likely hardships in adulting, and bring the pursuit home to a true definition of maturity.

—Dale Lunsford, PhD, President, LeTourneau University

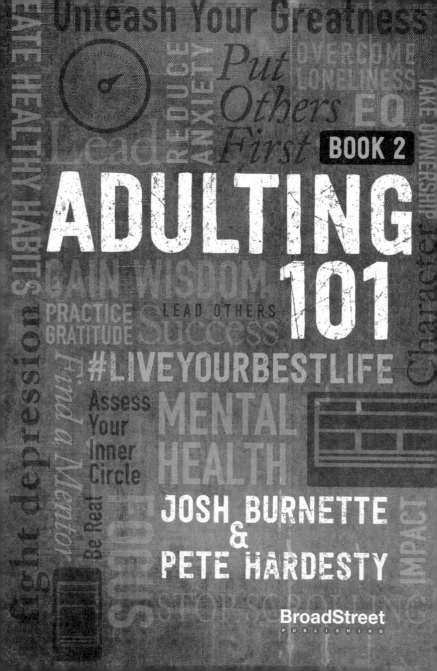

BroadStreet Publishing® Group, LLC
Savage, Minnesota, USA
BroadStreetPublishing.com

Adulting 101 Book 2: #liveyourbestlife
Copyright © 2021 Josh Burnette & Pete Hardesty

978-1-4245-6109-4 (hardcover)
978-1-4245-6110-0 (e-book)

Disclaimer: The purpose of this book is to provide helpful information around the areas discussed. The authors and publisher recommend you seek professional help as needed and cannot take personal responsibility for how the reader applies the information and its ultimate results.

Stock or custom editions of BroadStreet Publishing titles may be purchased in bulk for educational, business, ministry, fundraising, or sales promotional use. For information, please email orders@broadstreetpublishing.com.

Typesetting by Kjell Garborg and design by Chris Garborg | garborgdesign.com

Printed in China

21 22 23 24 25 5 4 3 2 1

CONTENTS

FOREWORD

In 2018, the song "Shallow" was made popular by the movie *A Star is Born*, starring Lady Gaga and Bradley Cooper. The song takes human form on-screen, and a complex love story with all the dignity and depravity our humanity can endure draws the viewer in. As with all songs that have this effect on me, I end up googling the lyrics to know the song more intimately, to understand why the piece resonates with me, and to appreciate its spark and depth. At times, I contemplate whether a part of it is applicable to my own life.

"Shallow" is about diving into love, into relationship, and into life—all with reckless abandon. There's a sense of predictability when diving into the deep end of a pool; you know it's safe to do. You're also simultaneously aware of the shallow end, and you consciously avoid diving into it. Imagine for a moment that "Shallow" is about you, your quest to find purpose, to fill the inner void, and to begin your journey to know yourself deeply. Would you dive in?

For twenty years, I have spent thousands of hours alongside young adults in my counseling office. Their experiences are wrapped in anxiety, fear, depression, sadness, confusion, loneliness, disconnection, and longing. Over the last two years, I have witnessed the severity, duration, and intensity of these negative emotions skyrocket. With strategic focus, *Adulting 101 Book 2: #liveyourbestlife* has the primary purpose of addressing anxiety, depression, and loneliness. This book comes at a crucial time in our culture.

Pete and Josh worked tirelessly on their first book, *Adulting 101*, to equip you with basic life skills. In this next book, they guide you into knowing and maintaining your inner self as a healthy adult. To dive into the depths of yourself requires only your willingness. That means asking introspective questions, reflecting on the answers, and taking deliberate steps to address negative emotions when they arise, either by confiding in a trusted friend, finding a mentor, or seeking professional help.

What you will discover in this book is a triad of principle, practical, and personal. Pete and Josh spent hours developing, supporting, and reiterating the principle that your life matters; you have greatness within you. You will find practical life applications, lists of questions, examples, and techniques that are both measurable and attainable. No point is belabored, and every chapter has direct, actionable, and helpful tools. The personal experiences throughout the book are relatable and provide opportunities to find common ground in adulthood experiences. You will learn how to prioritize and care for your mental health and foster your inner growth. It is a roadmap to adulting well.

Adulting 101 Book 2: #liveyourbestlife is a foundational resource to own. This book has a permanent home in my office and will be a gift to all my future twenty-something clients. May it provide you with the knowledge and wisdom to navigate adulthood with confidence. Dive deep.

Jonelle A. Frost, MA, EdS in Clinical Mental Health Counseling

INTRODUCTION

THE INNER QUEST TO ADULTHOOD

JOSH

It was literally a dark and stormy night. An epic thunderstorm shook the house, and howling wind blew so powerfully that the trees in the neighborhood started to bend. Cracks of thunder closely followed flashes of lightning. My toddlers had gone to bed a couple of hours earlier, and I prayed they would sleep through the storm. The only thing worse than a monstrous thunderstorm would be two toddlers screaming during a monstrous thunderstorm.

My wife had fallen asleep while we watched *The Office* in our room. When the episode was over, I decided to read for a little while. All of the lights in the house were turned off except the one on my nightstand. The storm continued to rage, and I eventually decided it was time to fall asleep. You know those moments when you think you've fallen asleep but aren't fully there yet? I had barely dozed off and felt my mind begin to dream when I heard my front door suddenly swing open. Why on earth was my door open? I shot up in my bed, now completely awake but startled, attempting to make sense of what I heard. Only one thought crossed my mind: someone was in my house. Nothing good comes from your front door flying open at eleven at night. In the five years we had been living in that house, our door had never opened by accident. I knew someone was in my house.

I jumped out of bed wearing only a pair of basketball shorts and ran toward the door. I didn't have a bat or weapon of any kind, but I followed my instinct to find the intruder. As I approached the front door, I saw it flapping in the wind. Rain poured into the house. Lightning flashed outside, and deafening roars of thunder rang in my ears. I searched the house, frantically checking room to room, but could not seem to find anyone. Ultimately, I concluded that no one was in my house, and my family was safe. But how did the door open?

Adulting often feels just as confusing and threatening as my experience during that memorable thunderstorm. We're launched into the season of adulthood feeling woefully unprepared, anxious, lost, and even terrified, wondering why we're still eating microwave burritos for breakfast. It's as if we wake up one day and start walking toward the future without a clue as to where we're going. We're adults in age, but we don't feel that way on the inside. We don't have a clear understanding of what to do or how to do it, and we lack the tools required to do the job well. If you feel this way, know that you are not alone. While it may not be as dramatic as a mysterious intruder in the middle of the night, the process of beginning to adult can be downright scary. This book will help you with that.

But first we want to admit that we wrote our books in the wrong order. This book should have been our first one, but better late than never, right? See, after Pete and I wrote the first *Adulting 101* book, we expected our families and friends to buy it and tell us it was good (even if they didn't believe that to be true). We figured they would be proud of us for giving it our best shot. But something different and entirely unexpected happened. *Adulting 101: #wisdomforlife* quickly became an Amazon best seller, and messages from young readers poured in telling us how much it helped them. Entire school districts even adopted *Adulting 101* as curriculum for their seniors. The response blew us away. We felt shocked and mystified. The response was way better than we could have imagined.

Of course, learning how to budget, land a job, rent an apartment, and buy a car are all crucial steps that most adults will take at one point or another. And while these responsibilities are undoubtedly essential, we also realized that we failed to address a hugely significant element to "adulting." Whereas our first book, *Adulting 101*, focused on the outside—finance, professionalism, prioritization, time management, dating—this book is all about adulting on the inside. In other words, our first book addressed *what an adult does*, and this book details *who a healthy adult is*.

The first book had a lot of answers. This one has a lot of questions.

The first book had a lot of advice. This one has a lot of reflection.

The first book had a lot of stories. This one does too. (Making sure you're paying attention!)

The first book was systematic. This one flows from topic to topic.

The first book was curated. This one is more raw.

"Adulting" T-shirts, mugs, phrases, books, magnets, and whatnot inundate our world. The concept has practically become part of our daily vernacular, and when you hear the word *adulting*, it's most often used in a negative context: "Adulting is hard" or "I don't feel like adulting today." What is it about being an adult that we don't feel like doing? Are we talking about the hard skills associated with adulting—taxes, health insurance, cars, and dinners that go beyond peanut butter and bread? Sure, these are tasks and responsibilities that we have to do post-school, but why do we so often associate adulthood with negative, less-than-enjoyable activities?

For starters, so many of us remain trapped in a constant pursuit of happiness. We convince ourselves that once we achieve happiness, life will make sense, and everything will finally be "good." And this pursuit of happiness starts young. It starts with getting good grades. Once we earn good grades, we'll be happy when those grades translate into acceptance to the best college. But once we're in college, happiness is keeping up those good grades because we all know that good grades in college mean that we'll land good jobs. And if we have a good job, then the right guy or girl will be attracted to us. Once we find the perfect someone to share life with, then we need adorable kids to be happy. And once we have those kids, happiness is getting those kids into the right school so that they, too, can have the best grades and get into the best college to have the best job and find the best spouse. Is this what life is all about? Is life just a perpetual rat race?

Striving for excellence is never a bad thing, but if you believe that accomplishing excellence will result in happiness and health, then you're setting yourself up for a lifetime of disappointment. Perhaps you don't find happiness in success, and perhaps life isn't about attaining happiness. We have all heard the stories of famous athletes, singers, CEOs, and actors who seem to cradle the entire world and all of its possibilities in the palms of their hands. They can buy or attain whatever they want because of their money, influence, and power. They're larger than life and, from all conventional societal measures, couldn't be any happier or more successful. And then they die by suicide. Or they enter rehab to treat an addiction. Or they experience a public meltdown that sends their career rushing down the drain. Or they disappear from the world's stage altogether. These heart-wrenching tales happen all too often. Many of these people grew up on the outside, which happens to every one of us, but missed the opportunity to mature on the inside.

Netflix released a documentary called *Miss Americana* about Taylor Swift, who is arguably one of the most successful artists of this millennium. In the documentary, she said, "You get to the mountain top and look around and go, 'What now?'" This was after she won Grammys in 2015 for "Album of the Year" and "Best Pop Vocal Album." She was at the zenith of the global music scene and felt empty inside. She had spent her entire life trying to be the best, assuming that professional success promised personal fulfillment. It was not until she realized that life had more to offer than success that she turned a corner and discovered who she truly was and what her passions were.

Stories like Taylor Swift's beg the question: Is there another path of adulting that's full of joy, adventure, satisfaction, impact, and fulfillment? We think so. In fact, we've found that the most common reason why so many young people resent adulthood is because they either don't know *how* to "adult" or simply don't *want* to know. They've never been set up to succeed. Oftentimes, those of us who have struggled with the transition to adulthood experienced at least one of three things:

1. We were not given a clear understanding of what adulthood means and how it applies to us.
2. We were not provided the necessary skill sets to know ourselves, lead ourselves, or know others.
3. We were not provided other critical resources, such as books and mentors, to set ourselves up for success.

There isn't a single adult on this planet who hasn't felt like their life was spiraling out of control or that they shuffled on shaky ground amidst a cloud of confusion. We are all unprepared to some degree.

Your twenties are the land of the in between. You are crossing the bridge from life as a student to life as a person in the workforce. You are likely moving away from casual relationships and instead pursuing a life partner. You leave home or your dorm to live in your first "real" place. You go beyond making important decisions to making decisions that can permanently alter the rest of your life. Your twenties can define the kind of adult you will become. How can you walk your path to becoming a healthy adult on the inside? To be able to handle whatever life throws at you? To be resilient? To be mature? To know yourself and know others? To provide value and change the world? To lead the life you were meant to live?

In *Adulting 101: #liveyourbestlife*, our purpose is to start you on the path to becoming a healthy adult on the inside. This will help you unleash your personal potential, inspire others to do the same, and equip you with the necessary skills to successfully adult. We also offer tons of additional resources and identify some of the consequences—both positive and negative—that come from being an adult.

We've broken this book into two major sections. Section One provides the expectations, skills, and resources for healthy adulthood. This includes how to know yourself, lead yourself, know others, and lead others, along with chapters on how to responsibly use technology and social media. Section Two walks through common challenges related to mental health that people experience in adulthood, including anxiety, depression, and loneliness. This second section also provides strategies from trusted mental health professionals to help you or someone you love overcome these challenges.

Becoming a healthy adult is a process that takes place over a period of time. It isn't a single moment or a destination. It is a journey with countless turning points, joys, and hardships. We hope that this book provides guidance for your adulting journey and helps you learn how to live the life you were meant to live: one of a healthy, fulfilled adult.

1

KNOW YOURSELF

PETE

Atlantic City. America's Playground. It's like Las Vegas—only dirtier. It is underpopulated in the winter and overpopulated in the summer. "Atlantic Ave" is a yellow space on the *Monopoly* game board, and it's actually named after Atlantic City. I was visiting this diamond in the rough with one of my best friends, whom we call Goody. He loves to dance so much so that he'll often drop it low even when there's no music. Or dance floor. And he'll do this entirely by himself. But this time in AC, he had music. We had just left a bathroom inside a casino when we saw a huge mirrored wall, probably twenty feet wide. Music played faintly in the background, so in true Goody fashion, he started dancing in front of the mirror, watching himself just crush it. Several people laughed as they walked by.

After a few minutes, we walked around the corner and were stunned to learn it had been a one-way mirror! Imagine the kind of mirrors you see in the movies or on TV during a police interrogation. On the other side of this mirror wasn't a bunch of detectives but a room dedicated to a casino game called Baccarat. A group of about twelve women were seated at two tables, and they had front-row seats to Goody's performance. They laughed hysterically. Goody sheepishly asked, "How did I do?" They applauded, but I think they might have been stretching the truth. Know thyself. Goody couldn't have an accurate understanding of how others perceived him because he was looking at a one-way mirror.

He had no idea what was *actually* going on or what others saw. How could he? He had no idea there was a whole other side.

According to the Greek writer Pausanias, the Ancient Greek aphorism "know thyself" was inscribed in the *pronaos* (forecourt) of the Temple of Apollo at Delphi.[1] Why should you know yourself? To stick with the Greeks, Socrates once said, "An unexamined life is not worth living." Why would this be true? Because a life without examination is severely limited. Without it, you cannot experience growth. Without growth, you can't have impact. In short, you can't fulfill your purpose without self-examination.

To truly know who you are is the most critical part in the foundation upon which your identity is built. Self-knowledge is not only the lens through which you see the world, but it is also the catalyst for your actions *in* the world. Know thyself. Know what you do. Know why you do it. Know how others receive it. Know what it's like to be on the other side of you. Know. Who. You. Are.

You were not meant to merely adult effectively but to have an impact. You have greatness inside you. Every person on earth does. It's part of the human experience. In fact, science tells us that every person has gold inside them (0.2 mg to be exact).[2] The highest concentration of gold is actually in and around the heart. And just like this gold, so, too, does everyone have greatness inside of them. It's a matter of seeing it and releasing it. Knowing yourself is the first step in releasing this greatness and becoming who you were meant to be. It's the beginning of your unique contribution to the world.

We will break down how to truly know yourself into three major parts. First, we'll define self-awareness. Then we'll identify influences that shape it and discuss the extent to which you can develop self-awareness. Lastly, we'll share practical ways to improve and build on it.

WHAT IS SELF-AWARENESS?

Self-awareness is defined as the "conscious knowledge of one's own character, feelings, motives, beliefs, and desires."[3] It's having a crystal-clear perception of who you are, complete with strengths, weaknesses, motivations, and emotions. It also means having an accurate picture of how others perceive you.

Many people believe self-awareness and emotional intelligence (EQ) are synonymous, but they're not. They are deeply related and interwoven but distinct concepts. Self-awareness focuses on recognizing what's going on inside of yourself and knowing who you are at your core. Emotional intelligence has more to do with how well you relate to others. We will take a closer look at emotional intelligence in a few chapters, so let's set that idea aside for now.

Think of self-awareness as the difference in experience between watching an epic movie on your phone and in an IMAX theater. I remember when the movie *Gravity* came out. It stars Sandra Bullock and George Clooney, and the film is set almost entirely in space. I distinctly recall one scene in which the screen goes pitch black with nothing but stars in the background. No sound. I was watching it in IMAX, so the gigantic screen surrounded me, and the silence swallowed me up. It momentarily transported me into space. I can't recall ever feeling more a part of a movie. But imagine watching that movie on your phone. Same movie, same words, same effects but a completely different experience. And a different outcome.

Developing self-awareness is like entering into an IMAX theater. You are still the same you, but you suddenly gain access to a limitless depth within yourself that propels you into a fuller, more authentic version of you. We are all on a quest to move away from the smartphone version of ourselves and replace it with the full color, surround sound, cinematic, IMAX version.

> *Knowing yourself is the most important thing you can do.*
> Neil Blumenthal, cofounder and CEO of Warby Parker[4]

Self-awareness first and foremost requires honest self-examination and reflection. It requires serious contemplation and a willingness to take risks with the people who know you best. Warning: it isn't always comfortable. Actually, it's almost never comfortable, and the process can be downright painful. We don't always like what we see. I sure didn't. Still, as challenging as it may be, it's worth the discomfort to know the truth and become stronger as a result.

Jeff Henderson, entrepreneur and thought leader, encourages self-awareness among his staff by asking them this question: "What's it like to be on the other side of me?" What he is actually asking is "How do I come across? What are my blind spots?" These are the things that everyone else knows about you *except* you. And when you don't know your blind spots, you lack an accurate picture of yourself. You can't see what you truly look like or understand how others perceive you.

Refusal or failure to discover and acknowledge your blind spots only makes them more powerful—and not in a good way. It's like stumbling your way through a funhouse of mirrors at a carnival. If you've never been inside a house of mirrors, it's basically a maze with walls made of mirrors that distort your reflection by making it appear smaller, larger, wider, narrower, further, and closer—to the point where you don't know right from left or up from down. Here's the good news about blind spots: everyone has them. And the bad news? Everyone has them. They're not easy to figure out, but with hard work, you can identify them and start to see what everyone else sees.

Self-awareness has value that goes far beyond yourself. It's the gift that keeps on giving. The more self-aware you become, the better leader you become, the better at motivating and investing in others you become, and the more "you" you become. The more you are able to fulfill who you were meant to be. An ideal workplace starts with self-awareness. An ideal family starts with self-awareness. An ideal romantic relationship starts with self-awareness. An ideal friendship starts with self-aware-ness. In turn, self-aware people make self-aware (better) employees, families, romantic partners, and friends.

MORE THAN "ONE IN A MILLION"

Be yourself. Everyone else is already taken.
Oscar Wilde, author

One of my best friends is a soccer fanatic. His name is Romesh, and he walked onto the University of Virginia's men's soccer team at the height of its dominance. The UVA men's team had won the national championship in 1989, 1991, 1992, 1993, and 1994—five out of six years. Romesh walked on in 1995, so he was good. Like, really good.

For his thirtieth birthday, Romesh and I traveled to England, and his incredible wife, Lawson, sent us to a Liverpool versus Arsenal soccer game (a Premier League football match). It was one of the best sporting events I've ever attended. Romesh thought it would be just the two of us for ten days. But to his surprise, three other friends joined us one by one. In England, one shrieked Romesh's name from a dark alley as we walked home from dinner. One hid in the shower in our rental flat in Notting Hill and jumped out when Romesh went into the bathroom to brush his teeth. That was a scary one. But the best reveal by far was his best friend, Danny. We were at a shawarma shop in Piccadilly Circus. It was cafeteria style, where you order your main dish, move down a long counter while selecting your sides, and then pay at the register. Danny was wearing the shawarma shop's uniform and standing at the register. In his best English accent (which was terrible), he asked Romesh, "Can I get you anything else?"

Romesh was flabbergasted. He shook his head, mumbling unintelligible gibberish. Then he let out a confused "Uhhh" as he turned to us in line and pointed at Danny. It looked like Danny, but Romesh thought it couldn't possibly be him. Romesh squeaked, "We have to take a picture." Romesh thought he had found Danny's twin.

It's often said that everyone has a twin somewhere in the world, but we wholeheartedly disagree. Vehemently disagree. Each one of us is unique. Even if we look very similar on the outside, each of us is our own person on the inside. We all have unique DNA—even identical twins![5] Your fingerprints, eyes, lips, tongue, and every other part of you are one-of-a-kind. Not only is your DNA—your "nature" or chemical makeup—unique, but your nurture is also unique. Your nurture includes your upbringing, culture, and life experiences. You've probably heard that you're "one in a million," but if that's true, then mathematically speaking that means there are almost eight thousand of you in the world since the world's population is approximately eight billion. In other words, "one in a million" isn't quite right. You're actually one in eight billion. There is no one like you. You have a specific purpose and a unique contribution to make.

If you've interviewed for a job recently, there is a good chance the interviewer asked plainly, "What makes you unique?" What *does* make you unique? The answer is actually quite a bit: your nature *and* your nurture. This includes your DNA, your motivations, your passions, your background, your experiences, your hopes, your dreams, and the lens through which you see the world are all unique to you. No one is exactly the same. What makes you tick and how you see the world are important concepts to explore and discover about yourself.

SHAPING INFLUENCES

"Where you stand is based on where you sit." This phrase is known as Miles Law, which is the idea that what you believe and how you see the world (where you stand) is deeply influenced by the culture and world in which you grew up (where you sit). This includes everything you ingest: the books, articles, and posts that you read, the podcasts and music that you listen to, the television and social media that you watch, and the mentors whom you allow to speak into your life. Major influences on your worldview and how you perceive yourself include your belief system, childhood, societal events, and your inner circle.

We don't see things as they are; we see them as we are.
Anaïs Nin, author

Belief System

Our values typically derive from our parents and whatever they believed (or didn't believe). This applies to religious beliefs as well. The Pew Research Center published an article in 2016 about the family impact on faith, and their conclusion was that students who grow up in a home of one religious background have the greatest likelihood of retaining those same beliefs into adulthood.[6] As a child, if you grew up in a household with parents whom you trusted, it makes sense that you would accept their beliefs as the only ones. You were too young to know much beyond that or make deeper decisions on your own.

As you launch into adulthood, this is a great time to evaluate what you believe and why. What did you accept as true because your parents or another trusted adult told you to believe? What have you accepted because it was "what everyone else believed" at the time? I have asked friends why they hold particular spiritual and political beliefs, and the wide range of responses has floored me. Their answers often come back to one of the two points mentioned above. Either they grew up in a household that believed it, or it is a culturally acceptable belief. Some just hadn't thought about it much. There is so much more to explore rather than accepting someone else's version of the truth.

Reflect on what you believe and why—for yourself. You can start with something small and silly, such as asking yourself what the best fruit is and why. For example, oranges are at the top of my list. They're easy to share, make a great breakfast, snack, or dessert, and provide delicious juice in the summer. The juice is definitely worth the squeeze. But usually we are talking about bigger, more meaningful, and often controversial topics, such as faith or politics. Or specific issues such as climate change, gun control, abortion, and immigration. Ask yourself what do you really believe, and why do you have this perspective? Your answers can reveal your values. It can also be helpful (and necessary) to engage in a respectful discussion with someone who holds beliefs opposite to yours. They may challenge you, and that's okay. Contrary to popular opinion, it's okay to disagree and have a civil dialogue about it, and it's also okay to change your mind.

Even your geography affects your belief system—everything from which side of town you came from, which state, country, and even which continent.[7] We cannot overestimate the roles that each of these elements play in the development of our perspective of the world.

Childhood

How you were nurtured and raised significantly influences your adult life. It provides you with your core beliefs about yourself, others, and the world. Amy Morin, author of *13 Things Mentally Strong People Don't Do*, wrote an article in which she states that your upbringing dictates what you think about everything else.[8] In short, if you had an overall positive childhood, you are more likely to believe that people are inherently good and that it is safe to trust others. But if you consistently experienced betrayal as a child, your ability to trust and believe in others as an adult is negatively impacted. A study by the University of Minnesota found that the level of nurture that you received by the age of three had an effect on your education, social life, and romantic relationships twenty or thirty years later.[9]

We can't stress enough that what happens in childhood affects you in a profound way, but it doesn't have to define you. In other words, growing up in a bad situation doesn't necessarily determine who you will become. Take *Gossip Girl* phenom Leighton Meester for example. Her story has gone mostly untold until recently. This talented and gracious actor was born behind bars while her mom served a jail sentence for smuggling 1,200 pounds of marijuana from Jamaica in 1983. Her aunt broke out of prison while serving time for this same crime and became the first woman to land on the US Marshals Most Wanted List. Leighton was separated from her mom for the first sixteen months of her life and then grew up in poverty. She said she "couldn't relate to normal kid stuff … I was worried about gas and food."

In 2012, Leighton ended her relationship with her mother following a bitter court battle that addressed claims that her mother allegedly extorted her daughter for money. The world came to love her as Blair Waldorf in *Gossip Girl,* but she is also a successful singer-songwriter, designer, and style icon. Meester shows us in a powerful way that your past and background affect you but do not need to define you. There is no "point of no return," and even with tragic, horrific beginnings, beauty can emerge. Understanding how your childhood has influenced you empowers you to address those issues, heal from them, and move forward.

Societal Events

The following story from Josh is a powerful illustration of how societal events shape our perspective of the world:

> I will never forget leaving my middle school class to go to the bathroom. I was walking through the halls and saw teachers talking in hushed tones around televisions. An eerie silence filled the hallways, which was atypical inside any school. Something was off. Shortly after returning to the classroom, my teacher explained that an airplane had hit one of the World Trade Center buildings in New York City.
>
> At the time, we thought it had been a tragic accident, but as the morning unfolded and the horrors of the day continued, I remember feeling deeply scared for my safety and my future. Parents picked up students to take them home as morning turned into afternoon. Feelings of uncertainty and fear swept the country. When I went home and watched the news with my parents that night, I, too, felt that fear. It was a knowing fear that something impacted me in a profound way but was wildly out of my control. On 9/11, my perspective of the world changed forever. I suddenly knew what a terrorist was, and I learned in living color just how evil humanity could be.

Every generation experiences an event that defines it and changes its understanding of life. For most millennials, 9/11 was that event. I remember watching the World Trade Center collapse, first thinking it was an action movie but quickly realizing it was really happening and was both terrifying and confusing. I had a college roommate who worked on the 101st floor of one of the towers. Doug was an incredible person. He was able to call his mom and talk for a minute before they lost the connection. He passed away in that terrorist attack. Our country has never been the same, and neither have I.

What major world events come to mind for you? Have you ever thought about how they might have impacted you? Growing up in the era of constant mass school shootings has given the current generation an outlook on guns and gun control that no other generation of Americans has previously experienced. Gone are the days of assuming that you will be safe at school, and that leaves a permanent impression. Perhaps the COVID-19 pandemic or racial justice protests of 2020 will be apex events for Gen Z. Remember that you are an infinitely complex person who has developed in the crucible of personal and worldly experiences and events.

Inner Circle

You will become the average of the five people you spend the most time with.
Jim Rohn, author of *The Art of Exceptional Living*

Your inner circle of friends is another crucial component in your self-awareness.[10] Your ride or dies. People who will love you and tell you the truth even when it hurts—especially when it hurts. Who will play the role of "lie detector" in your life? You need someone. They don't put up with fake or superficial. They don't hide your blind spots or encourage unhealthy behaviors or habits. They aren't scared of you. They speak to you from a place of love, and they encourage you to be the best version of yourself. They ask deep, probing questions. As author David John Seel explains, "We, too, need to build conscious contrarian voices into our leadership teams. … We need people around us to expose our pretense, self-importance, and inauthenticity."[11]

Here are a few questions to help you identify and assess your inner circle:

- Who are the five people you spend the most time with?
- Do they help you become the best you?
- Do they support you and your goals?
- Do they hold you accountable?
- Are they there for you when you need them? Would they drive you to the airport?
- Do you want to be more like them?

Your inner circle is dynamic. You are always growing and changing, so your inner circle may change as well. It may not. As your values change or others' values change, you might become incompatible. This is okay. It's a normal part of life and sometimes necessary, even if it is sad. It's not easy to drift apart from friends who were once close, but often, it is the natural byproduct of growing as a person.

WILLINGNESS TO CHANGE

Flight attendant: "If at any time we lose cabin pressure, oxygen masks will drop from the ceiling. *Please put on your own mask before helping others with theirs.*" Being intentional about increasing your self-awareness is like putting on your own oxygen mask when the plane loses cabin pressure. You put on your own mask and then help others with theirs. Because if you're not wearing one, then you're not going to be able to help anyone else. Self-awareness is that oxygen mask.

All of us are either trying to get better and change, or we are holding on tightly to something that is slowly dying and fading away. Continuous change is necessary if we want to learn and grow throughout our lives. To inspire ourselves to change, we must first overcome whatever denial we may have of who we are today. We can make a change by learning, reflecting, and fostering a desire to get better.

Robert E. Quinn, professor and author of *Deep Change*, writes, "The way to achieve and maintain excellence is to deviate from the norm. You become excellent because you are doing things normal people do not want to do. You become excellent by choosing a path that is risky and painful, a path that is not appealing to others."[12] According to Quinn, we have to be constantly moving and growing from what we consider "normal" in order for excellence to take root. This movement from the norm is difficult. You build the foundation of a healthy adult life on having a clear image of who you are. In a world full of filters and doctored images, vulnerability is key.

Without doing this difficult, exploratory, and developmental work, it's as if you're driving through life with the emergency brake on. I did this once and drove for almost an hour. My car was slow and unresponsive, and I didn't understand what was wrong. I started to get angry and frustrated, blaming my 1996 Jeep Cherokee. But it was user error. That is what we're like when we lack self-awareness and don't know ourselves. We are inhibited, impeded, and incapable of top performance.

HOW TO DEVELOP SELF-AWARENESS

Lots of influences shape your perspective of yourself, and it takes intentional effort to change. The great news is that wherever you fall on the spectrum of knowing yourself, you can improve! Here are some practical ways to boost your self-awareness.

Develop your inner circle (see previous section). You will become like these people, so choose them wisely. This process begins by deciding who you want to be. What qualities do you want to have? Whom do you connect with? Invest in and pursue people with those desired qualities.

Begin a journal. According to the *Harvard Business Review*, if you want to be an outstanding leader, then you have to journal.[13] If you've never done this before, try it once a day for two minutes. You can begin each entry with "Today, I …" if you prefer writing at night or "Yesterday, I …" if you're a morning person. Record the day's highlights and how you felt as the day progressed. Or record any observations you may have made about yourself or others. Record what is true of yourself. You can also find a ton of free journaling prompts online to guide your entries.

Utilize personality and strengths tests/assessments. These tools exist to help you understand your behavior, clarify your perspective of the world, and discover the true you. You want an accurate representation *of* yourself *to* yourself in order to discover why you react the way that you do. We recommend starting with the Enneagram[14] because it emphasizes your motivations, fears, and desires. It also sheds light on when you're operating in a healthy space versus an unhealthy space. Other helpful, reliable assessments include the Myers-Briggs Type Indicator, the StrengthsFinder, and the DISC. Many of these surveys have online versions available at no cost. As you learn about your tendencies and wiring, make sure that you use this information not as an excuse to remain how you are ("this is just how I am") but to empower your growth and facilitate your development.

Take relational risks. Ask for feedback from trusted friends. Ask them questions, such as, "What's it like to be on the other side of me? How do I come across? Do I have any blind spots?" While you listen to their answers, consider writing them down and reflecting on them. Avoid the temptation to defend yourself or justify your behavior. The only thing you're allowed to do is ask for clarification or examples if you want them. This is tough sledding, but it is worth it.

Develop your listening skills. Focus entirely on what a person is saying. Put yourself in their shoes and try to imagine their experience. Picture what they are saying. Try to understand what they are communicating and feel what they are feeling. Repeat back to them what you hear and ask questions. Offer verbal and physical feedback, like nodding and maintaining eye contact. Don't worry about what you are going to say next.

Listen for your inner voice. Is it positive or negative? What type of dialogue are you unconsciously having with yourself? On a scale from one to ten, how loud are the voices of other people in your life? What is the volume of your own voice? Decide to tell yourself only truth, encouragement, and affirmation. You have control over that inner voice. Remind yourself of at least one positive affirmation every morning.

Pay attention to what behaviors bother you in others. These can serve as signposts. Ask yourself if you ever do those same things. The imperfections we notice in others can be imperfections we see in ourselves. Or as psychologist Carl Jung said, "Everything that irritates us about others can lead us to an understanding of ourselves."

Read books and listen to podcasts on the subject of self-awareness. Brené Brown is a research professor and one of the world's leading experts in self-development. Her podcast, *Unlocking Us,* is excellent, and she has written several best-selling books that help us get to know and understand ourselves. She's also a Licensed Master Social Worker, so she specializes in mental health therapy skills and knowledge. Listening to her podcast or reading her books is basically free therapy.

Identify patterns in your reactions. Be on the lookout for moments when you experience disproportionate or inappropriate reactions or find yourself thinking, *Here we go again.* Those moments might shed light on behaviors that need improvement or resolution. For example, I realized that I had a need to be right whenever someone questioned me, particularly my title, position, or authority. Even on small issues, I always tried to "power up" and assert myself in a dominant way that would shut the other person down. I needed to win every argument. This is not good for relationships (trust me). It was—and still is—an insecurity of mine that stems from deriving too much of my value and identity from my position and performance. This was a warning light for something internal that was unresolved and needed work. Is there a subject, memory, or experience that you are particularly sensitive about? What makes you feel threatened or paralyzed? Let your answers guide you toward a better understanding of yourself.

BIG IDEA

Know thyself. You are a unique and creative being full of extraordinary talents and capabilities. It is time to uncover them. You have greatness inside of you, so unleash it. The more you grapple with and dig in to who you are, the better you can see who you were meant to become. With a proper understanding of yourself, you are equipped to launch into leading yourself more effectively.

2

LEAD YOURSELF

PETE

I want to tell you about a time when I was unwise. I mean really, really unwise. Downright foolish. Like eating-yellow-snow foolish. On his tenth wedding anniversary, one of my best buddies and his wife returned to Puerto Plata in the Dominican Republic, where they had enjoyed their honeymoon years earlier. They invited eighty friends and family members to join them at an all-inclusive resort, and about twenty-five of us were able to make the trip. It was a blast. One day, we wandered off the resort's property to a casino that was only about fifteen minutes away. (I realize that our first two chapters start with casino-related stories. It must seem like we spend a lot of time in them, but I promise this is purely coincidental. Cue nervous laughter.)

As soon as we walked into the casino, we received the gift of a fifty-dollar voucher to play a game called Crazy Eights, in which you roll dice and try to reach a certain total. I was playing with my best friend and his wife, who are two of the smartest, wisest people I know. We started off hot and almost hit the total within the first couple of rolls. If you hit the total, then you win the jackpot, which was around $100,000. I kept telling myself that if I could weather the storm, we would hit it big. I was convinced it was not a matter of *if* but *when*. The only problem was that with each roll, the player had to double their bet. The game escalated quickly, and the bets were soon in the thousands ... of dollars.

Never did I think this would ever be possible. I even had to break out a credit card to get a cash advance (this is never a good idea, but it's especially foolish when you're at a sketchy casino in a foreign country). I lost a *lot* of money that evening. We still think it was rigged, or at least, I hope it was. It was one of the most foolish things I've ever done, and I did it without the influence of drugs or alcohol. It was my own pure foolishness. Somewhere in the tropics is a person who still has my banking information, and they must laugh every morning as they sit on the beach, sipping a piña colada. But I learned from it.

The last chapter was dedicated to better knowing and understanding yourself. With that foundational understanding, the next challenge is to effectively lead yourself. The hardest person to lead is yourself. The hardest person to corral is yourself. You are 100 percent responsible for yourself. The common denominator in all of the decisions—both wise and foolish—that you've ever made is you.

Leading yourself requires several kinds of development. It requires understanding the difference between wisdom and knowledge. It requires learning to fail well and developing grit. It requires deliberate action in the forms of creating healthy habits, pursuing quality friendships, and seeking trustworthy mentors.

But before we dive into these topics, you need to be prepared. Learning to lead yourself well is difficult and takes time. You can run from people, places, and even situations, but you can never run from yourself. You'll always catch up. There are no quick fixes or shortcuts. There is no expedited shipping in which a new, empowered version of yourself arrives in two hours. But if you get going in the right direction, your life will begin to flourish.

WISDOM VERSUS KNOWLEDGE

To get wisdom is better than gold…more precious than rubies.
Ancient Proverb

Knowledge is information. It's facts. Currently, nearly all of the knowledge in the world is available at our fingertips. With a smartphone, we can find any obscure piece of trivia that anyone has ever wanted to know. Back in the day, people had to settle trivia disputes by either calling their smartest friend or by hauling massive, dusty encyclopedias off of their bookcase. Over the last forty years, knowledge has become a commodity. We no longer live in an age where we have to say "I don't know" about anything related to cold, hard facts.

Wisdom, on the other hand, is the synthesis and application of knowledge. It's the ability to make smart decisions and use discernment. It's making good judgments and knowing what is true and right. We gain wisdom from a complex combination of experience, humility, proactive learning, counsel, and reflection. What is the wise thing to do? This seemingly simple question can guide you to greatness and, when asked repeatedly over time, yield riches better than gold and more precious than rubies, at least according to an ancient proverb.

How do you determine the wise thing to do? How do you increase your wisdom and judgment? Confucius said, "By three methods we may learn wisdom: first, by reflection, which is noblest; second, by imitation, which is easiest; and third by experience, which is the bitterest." Here are twenty tips to help you gain wisdom.

20 TIPS TO GAIN WISDOM

1. Hang around wise people who you want to become more like.
2. Develop self-awareness (see chapter 1). Get to know yourself at your core and write down what is most important to you.
3. Stay humble. As Socrates said, "The only true wisdom is in knowing you know nothing."
4. Be open to new experiences. Take some risks.
5. Engage with people who have different views than you and remain open-minded during your conversations with them.
6. Read. Most all of us would rather watch Netflix, but reading opens your mind to new ideas and can change your perspective on all kinds of things. You can be mentored by anyone who has written a book! If you don't have time to sit down and read a book, try audiobooks or podcasts and listen to them while you

work out or drive. Pro tip: older, classic books are usually better than new releases. If a book has withstood the test of time, it is likely for a good reason. Something about it is worthwhile. If you are a person of faith, read your ancient wisdom literature.

7. Value and seek truth. It's easy to rely on social media or peers for news or updates, but make sure to check reliable sources and seek facts when forming your opinions on issues.

8. Think before acting. Pause before speaking. Take as much time as you need to deliberate on a problem before making a decision.

9. Learn from your mistakes. This is part of failing well. Our mistakes can be great teachers.

10. Suffer well. Need a powerful example of this? Read *Man's Search for Meaning* by Viktor Frankl.

11. Meditate or be intentional about spending time in silence and solitude. Pray for wisdom.

12. Reflect. Evaluate your feelings and actions at the end of each day, week, month, and year.

13. Pay attention to what you spend your time doing. Is it making you better? Is it guiding you in the direction you want to go?

14. Ask questions. Constantly. Pose them to yourself and others. A simple "Why?" is a perfect start.

15. Commit to a morning routine. (More on this in the next section.)

16. Cross-pollinate. Spend time learning about other people, cultures, and traditions.

17. Take control of your phone. Airplane mode is your best friend when you need a break.

18. Cultivate a habit of asking yourself, What is the wise thing to do in this situation? and What would a wise person do?

19. Use the HALT technique. Don't make important decisions when you are hungry, angry, lonely, or tired. Decisions made under these conditions often yield poor results.

20. Travel as much as possible. The more you explore, the more you expand your perspective.

CREATE HEALTHY HABITS

We are what we repeatedly do.
Excellence, then, is not an act, but a habit.
Will Durant, author of *The Story of Civilization*

Your habits determine the quality and direction of your life, so it makes sense to cultivate healthy ones. Healthy habits = healthy life. For example, we all know that if we exercise regularly (a healthy habit), we will have more energy, better sleep, and more clarity of thought (indicators of a healthy life). Several other habits receive less attention but are equally important when learning to lead yourself toward health. The first step in cultivating good habits is to reflect on your current habits. They are the silent partners in your life that determine who you are. What do you regularly watch, listen to, read, think, and say to yourself?[15]

The second step is intention. Practice makes perfect, right? Actually, not quite. Practice makes permanent. If you are practicing the wrong thing or doing something the wrong way, it ingrains a habit that is, at best, not helpful and even potentially harmful. Perfect practice makes perfect. You have to practice the right thing the right way. It's not simply the number of hours you put into something; it's what you do in those hours that is equally important.

So what makes perfect practice? Top performers seek out "just-manageable challenges, setting goals for practice sessions that just barely exceed their current capabilities."[16] That is half of the secret to optimizing performance. The other secret is complete focus on one thing. Total concentration (more on this in chapter 7).

A good place to start improving your habits is evaluating and revamping your morning routine. For some, this could be the single most important element in leading a more fulfilling life. What do you do in the morning? Is it consistent from morning to morning? Have you ever thought about it? Win the morning, win the day. That's what I've heard for a while. But is it true?

For most of my adult life, I never thought about my morning routine. I started out of college as a "snoozer" who hit the snooze button over and over. Looking back now, it seems insane that I chose to make myself miserable by waking up over and over again. I would sometimes reset my alarm for another half hour or hour or turn it off completely. Once I realized the importance of winning the morning, I took serious action. I moved my alarm clock all the way across the room. I instituted penalties if I snoozed. I even set the alarm for the last possible minute to make it to my first appointment in the morning so that I wouldn't have the option to snooze (I don't recommend this). But I still didn't think much about what I actually did in the morning.

About three years ago, I started thinking intentionally about my morning routine, and I've seen a tremendous difference. Instead of dreading mornings, I look forward to them because they help me focus and set me up for a successful day. They propel me to new levels of performance, accomplishment, and achievement. I still struggle with my evening routine, but I'm taking baby steps.

> *Lose an hour in the morning, and you will spend all day looking for it.*
> Richard Whately (1787–1863), Anglican archbishop

Master a Morning Routine

Your morning routine sets the stage for the rest of the day, and it actually begins the night before. If you stay up until two in the morning, then you are choosing to have a difficult morning the next day. In *The Wall Street Journal*, Nancy Jeffrey wrote, "It's official. Sleep, that rare commodity in stressed-out America, is the new status symbol. Once derided as a wimpish failing—the same 1980s overachievers who cried 'Lunch is for Losers' also believed 'Sleep is for Suckers'—slumber is now being touted as the restorative companion to the creative executive mind."[17] We need sleep, and we all know how hard it is to wake up early and do the things that we need to do when we're exhausted.

In addition to getting good sleep, we highly recommend trying some type of meditation. In *Tools of Titans* and *Tribe of Mentors*, Tim Ferriss asked world-class performers in various industries a series of questions, and almost every single person mentioned meditation as a crucial part of their routine. Why? Research shows that regular meditation helps alleviate stress and anxiety. This valuable time also naturally engages you in self-awareness and allows you to internally process areas of your life in need of improvement.

Finally, consider adding a workout to your morning routine. I have a friend who does intense workouts first thing in the morning. He wants to break a sweat before dawn and says he likes to put himself through the toughest part of his day first: "Nothing else I face for the rest of the day will be as hard as that." That's admittedly not my style. I prefer to exercise after reading, writing, meditation, and prayer. My workouts aren't as difficult as his either, and that's okay. Not everyone's morning routine has to look the same.

The point is to infuse healthy habits into your life while you're young. Find your rhythm. What does your ideal morning look like? What time will you wake up? What time do you need to go to bed? How do you want to use this time? Write it down in an app on your phone or in a notebook. It doesn't have to be perfect. It's a work in progress that you can revise as you experiment and learn.

One important thing to note is that your routine might look different depending on what season of life you're in. If you are in your first year out of high school or college, you might have flexibility in creating a longer, more robust morning routine. If you recently had your second child, your morning routine might only allow six minutes, most of which are taken up by changing diapers and preparing bottles. Your routine can be six minutes or sixty. It's up to you.

Contrary to popular belief, productivity isn't about how much you can do.
It's about whether or not you're doing the right things...
and that means starting small with what you know matters to you.
Melissa Steginus, author of *Self Care at Work*

The first step to crafting your routine is to make it as systematic and ritualized as possible. The fewer decisions you have to make in the morning, the better. Set an alarm that goes off at the same time every day. Lay out your clothes the night before, and if you're going to exercise, lay out your athletic clothes too. I know people who even sleep in their exercise clothes so that they're ready to go first thing in the morning. And when you wake up, try not to look at your phone. Instead, wait to look at your phone until you begin your work day. If that's not doable, at least try not to let it be the first thing you do. The longer you spend your morning without your phone the better your day will be.

Next, follow the wisdom of Navy Admiral William McRaven: "If you want to change the world, start off by making your bed."[18] Studies agree and have shown that making your bed actually makes you more productive.[19] This simple act begins your day with an accomplishment, regardless of how small it may be. Then choose positivity. Author Jon Gordon says we have two choices in the morning: rise and shine or rise and whine.[20] Make the choice to shine and start your day with gratitude, not helplessness. In a journal, planner, or on a piece of scratch paper, write down five things that you're thankful for. This can be a game-changer and determine your attitude and perspective for the day.

Most importantly, give yourself grace. If you mess up your routine on any given morning, the best part is that another one is right around the corner. Let's say you design a morning routine but only implement it once during your first week. One morning is better than none. Keep at it.

In the back of this book, you'll find my detailed morning routine and Josh's, as well as a sample evening routine. I developed mine over the course of about a month by asking myself, *What does my ideal morning look like?* Much of the structural inspiration comes from Hal Elrod's book *Miracle Morning*. Of course, these routines are flexible and customizable. They can last ten minutes or two hours. For example, while we wrote this book, I dedicated more time to writing and less time to reading.

Do we accomplish our routines every morning? Nope. We probably succeed at it three to four mornings per week. Still, that's better than zero. If you're interested in other people's insight on morning routines, check out Michael Hyatt, Enuma Okoro, Tish Harrison Warren, Jocko Willink, Hal Elrod, Tim Ferriss, and Ruth Haley Barton.

HOW TO FAIL WELL

Failing well. Two words that aren't ordinarily paired together, especially if you are a perfectionist like Josh:

I hate failing, but I'm getting pretty good at it these days. If the definition of failure is not accomplishing what you set out to accomplish, then I have been doing that my entire life. However, I also believe that there is far more to learn from failure than success. You don't learn nearly as much when you are successful, and rarely do you retroactively try to understand why success even took place. Most of the time, we simply move on to the next task to accomplish.

I used to believe in a single plan for my life, and I was consumed with trying to make that plan unfold exactly how I wanted. I had an impossibly narrow definition of success and was convinced that if I picked the right school, the right spouse, the right career, the right city, then I was sure to accomplish my plan for my life. Instead, I failed at getting into the college I wanted (actually the top three colleges I wanted), dating the girl I was close to in college, securing the job for which I trained for eight years, and landing a career in the city I wanted to live. Just about everything in my adult life has materialized differently than the way I had hoped. And you know what? Those "failures" were exactly what I needed to grow, and they brought me to the place where I am today. I am truly glad to have failed at each of those experiences.

Winners are not afraid of losing. But losers are. Failure is part of the process of success. People who avoid failure also avoid success.
Robert T. Kiyosaki, entrepreneur, author of *Rich Dad, Poor Dad*

Tony Bennett, the University of Virginia men's basketball coach, had a mediocre record of 15–16 in 2009, his first season at UVA. He kept improving, little by little, and worked up to a record of 31–3 by the 2017–2018 season. That same season, he suffered the worst loss in college basketball history during the 2017–2018 NCAA tournament, becoming the first number-one seed in their bracket to lose in the first round. For context, the March Madness number one seed had gone 132–0 up until that season. The very next year, Bennett coached the underdog UVA team to win the national championship. He was awarded the Associated Press's "National Coach of the Year" award and now boasts the highest winning percentage of all time at the University of Virginia.

The reality is that there isn't one right plan for your life; there is a purpose. And whether you graduated from Harvard or dropped out of high school, as long as you pursue your purpose, the details unfold exactly how they need to. Do not mistake failure as missing out on your life plan. Failure is necessary and useful. You will continue to fail for as long as you are alive, so learning how to successfully fail is one of the most valuable skills that you can acquire. It is one of the many things that make you human. One of my mentors would say: "Get comfortable with failure but get better because of it." Here are some tips from *Relevant Magazine* on how to handle failure successfully:

- "Put it all out there." Whatever you do, go after it 100 percent. Don't let failure prevent you from committing to do your best.

- "Don't let failure make you bitter." This is the hardest one. I have been passed up for opportunities within my organization at three times the rate that I have been accepted. It would be easy to take the failure as a personal attack that I am not good enough. But that isn't the reality. I am not a failure. Those opportunities were not part of the purpose of my life.
- "Don't let failure become final." It isn't the end of the world. Keep moving forward! Don't let an unexpected outcome define you.
- "Learn and grow from failure." Failure is one of the greatest lessons in adulthood. If we can learn from our mistakes, we become more well-rounded adults.[21]

Walt Disney was fired from a Missouri newspaper in his early twenties for "not being creative enough." Over the next couple of years, two other animation companies he founded went bankrupt. But he didn't stop trying. The gaming company Rovio created fifty-one games, all of which failed. They were on the verge of bankruptcy when they released their fifty-second game: Angry Birds. It was a smash hit with over a billion downloads and even led to the production of a full-length feature film.

All the adversity I've had in my life, all my troubles and obstacles, have strengthened me … You may not realize it when it happens, but a kick in the teeth may be the best thing in the world for you.
Walt Disney

Lebron James has made nineteen game-winning shots in the final seconds of NBA games, but he's missed twenty-seven. Lebron, Kobe, and Jordan (possibly the three best basketball players ever) have all missed more buzzer beaters than they made. They failed more than they succeeded. Colonel Sanders of KFC (Kentucky Fried Chicken) fame tried to sell his fried chicken recipe over a thousand times and was rejected. It wasn't till the 1010th time that someone took a chance on it. Lady Gaga, now one of the world's best-selling music artists, first signed a record deal with Def Jam at age nineteen but was let go after just three months. The label didn't think she had talent or a future, but she pressed on, signed with a different label, and produced her first debut album, which topped the music charts in several countries. Our point is that anything good will be hard. Anything meaningful will require failure. The seeds of greatness are planted in the soil of failure.

I've embraced fear and failure as a part of my success. I understand that it's part of the grand continuum of life.
Viola Davis

It's frustrating when you set out to do something and fail. You go all out for the big promotion or for the person you believe is "the one." In those moments, take a deep breath, be frustrated, but then get up, do a little soul searching, learn from the experience, and move on. Greatness is not perfection; it's the willingness to keep going.

DEVELOP GRIT

Mentally strong people don't metaphorically dust themselves off and get right back on their horse. They pause to figure out why they fell off in the first place before getting back on.
Amy Morin, author of *13 Things Mentally Strong People Don't Do*

"No one will outwork me." I lived by this mantra for a long time. Where did this come from? I think a big factor was my dad. He grew up with limited financial resources, put himself through college and then medical school, and is one of the hardest workers I've ever known. He left for work early in the morning and came home right before dinner. When my parents were cleaning out their crawlspace, they found a box of my dad's old school papers. One of them was an autobiography from eleventh grade that he had typed on a typewriter, which I've heard are notoriously difficult to use without making errors (imagine not having the convenience of a "backspace" or "delete" button). It only had two typos! With no autocorrect! In his autobiography, my dad wrote about two factors that shaped him most as a person: his parents' divorce when he was twelve and the eighteen facial plastic surgeries he endured during his first seventeen years of life because of a severe birthmark. He had to work hard and persevere to overcome these challenging obstacles. He is the definition of grit.

I have felt less gifted than those around me, especially when it comes to sports. I would compensate for my lack of athletic ability with hard work and hustle. In basketball, I was the scrappy guy diving after every loose ball, pushing myself to the brink. For soccer, I conditioned myself to have the endurance to go all out for an entire game. I knew I needed that edge to compete. This developed into an unhealthy, workaholic attitude when I started working as an adult. I lived by the idea that you could outwork any problem. I would email someone late at night and then again first thing in the morning to give the illusion that I never stopped working (I know … I have problems). I wore my hard work like a badge of honor. But it was also an addiction and the only one I know of that gets you ahead in life. The only one for which people pat you on the back and wink. It's true that success cannot take place without hard work. And while hard work doesn't solve every problem, few problems are solved without it. What I needed was grit. Grit is the healthy version of going the extra mile.

Dr. Angela Duckworth wrote a remarkable book aptly titled *Grit* that's dedicated to this very idea. One of the biggest challenges for young people is their environment. We live in the age of instant. Instant meals, books, relationships, communication, work, travel, clothes, etc. The faster, the better. This has produced a recurring dilemma for young people. They want to advance quickly in work and in life but become rapidly frustrated when that doesn't happen fast enough. Ambition is great. Talent is helpful, but grit is the game-changer. Grit matters more than talent, and it's something we can cultivate.

Let's play a round of "Guess Who?" Here are clues to a well-known historical figure:

- His mom died when he was nine years old.
- His twenty-year-old sister died in 1828.
- He failed in business in 1831 and again in 1833.
- He was defeated for state legislature in 1832.
- He ran for Congress twice and lost both times in 1843 and 1848.
- He tried running for the Senate twice and lost both times in 1855 and 1859.
- He ran for Vice President and lost in 1856.
- Two of his sons died as children.

Who might this be? In 1860, he signed his name A. Lincoln and was elected President of the United States. Now *that* is grit.

> *The difference between history's boldest accomplishments and its most staggering failures is often simply the diligent will to persevere.*
> Abraham Lincoln

Most all of us have set a new goal that we felt super motivated to accomplish. We are going to train for that marathon, read that book, or lose those pounds. But shortly thereafter, we lose steam, and our excitement fades into the background. This is what happens with just about every New Year's resolution. Eighty percent of New Year's resolutions fail by February.[22] Eighty percent of people who join gyms in January quit within five months.[23] We need grit to persevere.

Grit consists of two primary elements: passion and perseverance. As Dr. Duckworth wrote, "Enthusiasm is common. Endurance is rare."[24] Grit isn't sexy or exciting. It means showing up and working hard day in and day out. Nothing happens instantly. But with a little bit of grit, you can achieve far greater results than simply being talented. In fact, throughout her studies, Dr. Duckworth surveyed thousands of people, and here is what she discovered: "In sharp contrast, you can see that grittier people are dramatically more motivated than others to seek a meaningful, other-centered life. Higher scores on purpose correlate with higher scores on the Grit Scale."[25] Nothing great in life comes without great sacrifice. Here are four simple tips for developing grit and getting things done:

1. Decide what the most important task is for the day and attack it first. If you have a tendency toward action, it is amazing how much gets done when you prioritize this way.

2. Beginning a task is often the biggest hurdle. I put "start _____" on my to-do list instead of "finish." It is surprising to me how different that can feel. It's also surprising how simple some tasks are when you actually start them.

3. Commit to doing one hour of focused, hard work on something that feels overwhelming. Set a timer for an hour and just start. It's okay if you don't finish. You have to start somewhere.

4. Share your deadline with another person and tell them that you will check in with them once you complete the task. This simple act of creating accountability for yourself can be a huge help.

PURSUE QUALITY FRIENDSHIPS

Everything that we have talked about in this chapter so far has been an internal motivation. Arguably, these final two elements can have even greater impacts on leading yourself well. They have to do with surrounding yourself with the right people. This means pursuing quality friendships and finding a group of mentors. Throughout the remainder of this chapter, we will discuss the importance of these core relationships, and later in this book, we will dig deeper into how to foster them.

Friends matter. Take it from Josh, who saw this principle play out vividly in college:

As a freshman, I moved into a random dorm like most all the other five thousand freshmen on James Madison University's campus. It was an exciting time to try different things, make new friends, and live on my own. It was the most freedom I had ever felt, and I loved it. So did my friend Sean from high school.

Sean was a smart young man who did well in high school, but college was an entirely different challenge. He struggled with building close relationships because each time he made a friend, he clung to that person so tightly that he exhausted the relationship altogether. So he joined a sports team as a manager and made friends that way. While his motives were good, the environment wasn't healthy for him. His new friends did not share his values or interests, nor did they build him up or help him become the best version of himself. They were not inherently bad people or out to get him, but Sean felt lonely and defeated. By the middle of his junior year, he was on the verge of a breakdown.

Instead of intentionally pursuing friendships with people who genuinely cared about him, Sean had settled for friendships of convenience. He never sought out other activities, opportunities, or people, and he ended up spending all of his free time with the same people from the team. He was unable to see the negative impact these relationships were having on his life. He gave up on himself and believed he was the victim of his empty friendships.

I am profoundly grateful to have had a different experience. I sought out friendships with people whom I desired to become more like. During my sophomore year, I moved into a house full of other young men who were involved in the same nonprofit as me. We didn't agree on everything, but we shared a foundational core belief system, and from that, profound friendships sprouted. When I looked around that house, I wanted to be more like this group of guys. They were smarter, more intentional in their relationships, and knew who they were as individuals.

My friend group inspired me. These men propelled me to ask deep questions and pushed me outside of my comfort zone in a healthy way. They challenged me to become a better student, a better friend, and a better man. They helped me grow. I grew more as a person during my three years of living in that house than perhaps any other period in my life. Many of the guys I lived with were in my wedding and are still some of my closest friends today.

It's been said that "your friends will determine the quality and direction of your life," so it's crucial that you pursue and maintain quality friendships in order to enjoy a healthy adult life.[26] In short, who you decide to surround yourself with will drive many of your future decisions. Some of us may feel like we got involved with the wrong crowd early on or made poor decisions that we regret. If that was your high school, college, or post-grad experience, it's okay. Starting life as an adult is a great time to reevaluate what you consider to be important in friendships and to start fresh. It's never too late to find good friends. It takes work, and you will likely have to step out of your comfort zone, but healthy friendships are worth all the effort that it takes to find them.

Finding friends does not happen by accident in most cases. To find good friends, you first must become a good friend. It takes initiative. It's also important to identify the qualities and traits that you want to find in others, especially those with whom you spend the most time. Here is a short list of questions to ask yourself:

- Do you share common interests?
- Do you have similar values?
- Can you trust them?
- Do they listen and ask you questions, or do they only talk about themselves?
- How do you feel after being with them?
- Are they optimistic or pessimistic?
- Are they unnecessarily dramatic or constantly having issues that absorb the entire relationship?
- Do they genuinely care about you?
- Do they respect your beliefs and boundaries?

Keep in mind the value of spending time with people who are also different from you. You can learn so much from people who have completely different life perspectives than yours, whether that's related to gender, race, socioeconomic level, faith, and more. Our focus in this chapter is to point out that you need a couple of close friends in your life who share the same values and goals because they can build you up, hold you accountable, and make you better.

SEEK OUT A CONSTELLATION OF MENTORS

All mentors have a way of seeing more of our faults than we would like. It's the only way we grow.
George Lucas, creator of the Star Wars franchise

As you think about leading yourself, remember that you're not the first person to do it. That's why mentorship is so important. Think of a mentor as a coach. Every great athlete needs a coach. Even LeBron needs a coach. The goal of mentorship is to find someone who is a little bit ahead of you in an area of life, be it career, finances, faith, marriage, parenthood, or something else. A mentor is someone you admire and aspire to become like. Don't limit yourself to one because that leaves all of your eggs in one mentor basket. All of the high capacity people I know have several mentors, a constellation of mentors if you will. No one excels in every aspect of life, which is why high performers secure a variety of mentors to support them in different areas.

Josh has a professional life coach who helps him become a better business leader, husband, dad, and member of his community. His coach knows that their relationship exists to give Josh encouragement in areas where he can improve, share honest feedback with him, and help him accomplish his goals. Josh says this relationship is invaluable.

A mentor can also provide visibility into your blind spots. Initially, this may feel uncomfortable. It's easy to feel offended by some of your mentor's feedback. But having someone who is a step ahead of you who can also provide insight into your personal life is so worthwhile. Leading business site and magazine *Inc.* published an article in 2016 about the importance and value of a mentor. Here are their top ten reasons for getting a mentor:

1. Mentors provide information and knowledge.
2. Mentors can see where we need to improve where we often cannot.
3. Mentors find ways to stimulate our personal and professional growth.
4. Mentors offer encouragement and help keep us going.
5. Mentors are disciplinarians that create necessary boundaries that we cannot set for ourselves.
6. Mentors are sounding boards so we can bounce ideas off them for an unfiltered opinion.
7. Mentors are trusted advisers.
8. Mentors can be connectors.
9. Mentors have the experiences you can learn from to prevent making the same mistakes beginners make.
10. Mentors are free, which makes them priceless in more ways than one.[27]

Remember, mentors don't show up and fix all of your problems. Finding a mentor means that you have to take initiative and put effort into maintaining the relationship. They are the coach, and you are the athlete. They can tell you what to do to get better, but it's up to you to do the work.

How do you find a mentor? The first step is identifying what area(s) of your life you want to grow or develop. Is it your career trajectory, your character, a certain skill? Knowing your short and long-term goals will help clarify what kind of mentor you want. Start by looking inside your workplace and within your network. Who do you look up to? Think personally and professionally. If you've already established a relationship with someone, the asking part becomes easier.

Begin by setting up a time to grab coffee and see if there's a connection. Keep it casual. If all goes well, schedule a second meeting and be prepared to share clear goals as to what you hope to develop or improve. Clarity is key. Nothing is more frustrating for a mentor than someone who asks for development but cannot articulate what that looks like or express their objective. Take notes during your meetings and ask thoughtful questions. Ask for feedback. The point of the relationship is for you to learn and improve. If your mentor avoids tough conversations, then you found a cheerleader, not a mentor. Follow up afterward with phone calls or meetings. Lastly, make sure to thank them regularly for their time.

The most important person you will ever lead is yourself. You are the most complex puzzle you will ever have to solve. The good news is you are not flying blindly. You are uniquely positioned to know yourself and lead yourself better than anyone else. You were made for this. Keep putting those puzzle pieces into place one at a time as you develop the beautiful mosaic of you.

BIG IDEA

Knowing how to lead yourself is both an internal and external journey. You need to know who you are and who you want to be in order to lead yourself effectively. The five components to leading yourself we discussed in this chapter are building blocks to help you move from knowing and leading yourself to knowing and leading others.

3

KNOW OTHERS

PETE

Have you ever looked around and thought, *Uh oh, I misread this situation. Badly.* Has anyone ever told you, "You don't understand where I'm coming from"? If you regularly feel surprised or blindsided by the feelings and reactions of others, then this chapter is for you. Or if you're already in control of your emotions and possess a natural ability to perceive the emotions of others, this chapter will help you hone your craft.

I would like to share a time when I completely misread a situation. Between you and me, it's honestly one of many. I was living in Harrisonburg, Virginia, where I had the privilege of helping James Madison University start a chapter of the nonprofit organization called Young Life College. We were in the experimental phase, holding events to see what worked and what didn't. The next year, we felt like we had a good idea of what to do, but we overextended ourselves. Actually, I overextended our small but mighty volunteer leadership team made up of six incredible college students and one incredible professor. At the beginning of the semester, we hosted what we called "Welcome Week," during which we held an event every day or night for ten consecutive days. We hosted a dance party, organized and started small groups, and then culminated the week by bringing more than one hundred students on a weekend retreat.

During our first team meeting after Welcome Week, I felt so pumped about our start to the year that I brought bottles of sparkling cider and fun champagne flutes to celebrate our success with a toast.

But as I pulled out the bottles and glasses, the record scratched, and the room went silent. I looked up to furrowed brows, dark circles under eyes, and even a couple scowls that bordered on downright glares. *Uh oh*, I thought. Something was amiss. I opened up the floor for reflection and sharing and asked how everyone was doing. They told me how tired they felt and said they had been pushed to the brink. They were frustrated, exhausted, angry, and resentful. I sheepishly tried to slide the cider and champagne flutes back into my bag, but it was too late. The cat was out of the bag. Or really, the Welch's grape juice was out of the bag. I had misled our team and then misread them. I blew it.

> *The greatest of faults is to be conscious of none.*
> Thomas Carlyle (1795–1881),
> author of *On Heroes, Hero-Worship, and the Heroic in History*

My blunder with the Young Life College team is an example of a blind spot. I frequently demonstrate low EQ, which, as previously noted in chapter 1, is an abbreviation for emotional quotient but more commonly known as emotional intelligence. Have you ever been surprised or even shocked by how people react or perceive reality? At work, can you consistently sense how your coworkers are feeling? Thankfully, my team graciously gave me a second chance, and I learned (with more practice) the rhythms of the semester and how best to lead them.

Sometimes our blind spots make good teachers. For example, my lack of EQ taught me the necessity of rest. After all, you can't sprint for ten miles. This idea reminds me of a line from *The Bourne Identity* in which the main character, Jason Bourne, says, "I know the best place to look for a gun is the cab of the gray truck outside, and at this altitude, I can run flat out for a half mile before my hands start shaking." Do you know how far you can run before you break down? That's knowing yourself. Do you know how far your team can run before they break down? That's knowing others.

To become a healthy adult, you must develop both emotional

intelligence and emotional maturity. EQ "is the understanding of human emotions—your own and those to whom you relate."[28] Emotional maturity is "how well you are able to respond to situations, control your emotions, and behave in an adult manner when dealing with others."[29] It is the application of emotional intelligence. In short, you first must have emotional intelligence in order to develop emotional maturity.

WHAT IS EQ?

Here's a more robust definition of EQ: "From a scientific standpoint, emotional intelligence is the ability to accurately perceive your own and others' emotions; to understand the signals that emotions send about relationships, and to manage your own and others' emotions."[30] It is the capacity to be aware of, control, and express one's own emotions. It is how we perceive people and how people perceive us, how we experience people and how they experience us. This extends to our home life, work life, love life, family life, and really *all* aspects of life. It was popularized by author Daniel Goleman in his book *Primal Leadership*. In it, Goleman breaks EQ down into four skills. The first two domains are personal competence and the second two are social competence:

1. Self-awareness: reading your own emotions and knowing yourself. We talked a lot about this in chapter 1: Know Yourself.
2. Self-management: self-control, honesty, adaptability, flexibility (chapter 2: Lead Yourself)
3. Social awareness: empathy, organizational awareness on a bigger scale (chapter 3: Know Others)
4. Relationship management: compelling vision, developing others, catalyzing change, teamwork (chapter 4: Lead Others)[31]

WHY CARE ABOUT EQ?

Research shows convincingly that EQ is more important than IQ in almost every role and many times more important in leadership roles.
Stephen Covey[32]

Many believe EQ to be the single most effective predictor of professional and personal success. And for good reason. Studies have shown that people with high emotional intelligence have greater mental health, better job performance, and stronger leadership skills. Students who can manage their emotions do better and get farther in life.[33] EQ can even predict academic performance.[34] A thirty-year study in New Zealand noted every child born in Dunedin and followed their progress into their thirties. One factor predicted financial success better than any other factor, including IQ and family income. You guessed it! It was EQ.[35] This outcome makes sense because so much of what we do in our academic, personal, and professional lives involves people. It's how we see, lead, live with, talk to, and understand people.

James Heckman, Nobel Prize winner and founder of the University of Chicago's Center for the Economics of Human Development, says that differences in incomes are only 1–2 percent attributed to IQ.[36] He says the two key factors in predicting income are EQ and personality, which are integrally related. Ninety percent of top performers are high in emotional intelligence.[37] They have learned the secret to controlling their emotions and putting them to work by letting their emotions follow, not lead, their actions. *Emotions are great friends but terrible masters*. So how do we make our emotions our friends instead of our rulers? Is emotional intelligence something we can improve?

Do you want the good news or the bad news first? I knew you would pick the bad news. Everyone does. The bad news is that EQ is a gift. Some people are naturally wired to see "inside" people and intuitively know how to persuade and influence others. We all have a friend like this. They're super perceptive and can always tell when something's going on with you, even when you think you're hiding your heartache. The good news is that EQ is also a skill, not a fixed capacity. Several studies have shown that EQ can be increased, developed, built, explored, and improved. You can grow your emotional intelligence in several ways. Let's highlight some of the critical ones that tend to have the greatest impact. We've also included a list of thirty of the best questions to ask in order to get to know someone in the appendix at the end of the book.

> *Human beings, by changing the inner attitudes of their minds,*
> *can change the outer aspects of their lives.*
> William James[38]

Positive Self-Talk

Saturday Night Live once had a super popular skit called "Daily Affirmations with Stuart Smalley." It was tongue-in-cheek and poked fun at self-talk. Stuart would look in the mirror and affirm himself daily, saying, "You're good enough, you're smart enough, and doggone it, people like you." We laughed, but it turns out there's something to this.

See, our perspective and perception dictate the bulk of our emotional intelligence: "To change one's emotions … we must change the way we perceive and think about events and, to the best of our ability, through better thinking, prevent the flow of stress hormones into our bodies."[39] Easier said than done, right? If we don't want to become instantly furious when someone cuts us off in traffic, then we have to change the way we think about being cut off in traffic, which means we have to change our perception of other drivers and choose our reactions. Instead of flying into a rage and tailgating the reckless driver, we can choose to take a deep breath, recognize that this driver's poor decision was not personal (even if it feels like it was), and decide that getting upset over a minor injustice simply isn't worth our energy.

Not only do we need to change the way we perceive and think about events in order to develop our EQ, but we also need to change the way we perceive and think about ourselves. More specifically, we have to learn to leverage an emotional language that all of us already speak: self-talk. Our self-talk has incredible power over our emotions as well as our actions, which is precisely why we need to observe, understand, and challenge our self-talk and decide how we will speak to ourselves.[40]

Consider your inner monologue for a moment. What do you tell yourself when facing a challenge? Do you think, *I've got this; my whole life has prepared me for this*, or do you tell yourself you can't do it because you're not smart, athletic, or attractive enough? Self-talk has a self-ful-filling power. If you're constantly telling yourself negative, harmful things, you come to believe them. On the other hand, if you develop the habit of speaking positive, affirming, and empowering things, you come to believe them and act accordingly. Positive self-talk works. It helps us take control of our next action and even our next emotion.[41] We must learn to speak positively to ourselves in times of tension and distress as well as in times of peace and focus.

> *Whether you think you can, or you think you can't—you're right.*
> Henry Ford, founder of the Ford Motor Company

Put Others First

Robin Dreeke was head of the FBI's Behavioral Analysis Program and has studied interpersonal relations for more than twenty-seven years. Here's Dreeke's number-one piece of advice for building rapport with people: "Seek someone else's thoughts and opinions without judging them."

Ask questions. Listen without judging. No one likes to feel judged, and you can validate someone without agreeing with them. Dreeke also mentions that he loves to ask people about challenges: "What kind of challenges did you have at work this week? What kind of challenges do you have living in this part of the country? What kinds of challenges do you have raising teenagers?" Everyone has challenges, and they can be a window into people's priorities and help you understand what is important to them.[42]

When getting to know others, we need to shift from self-obsession to others-obsession. We must be interested in people instead of trying to be interesting ourselves. Try to ignore the gravitational pull to insert your story, your witty comment, or your opinion. Instead just listen. Choose to serve, no matter how you feel on the inside. Set others up to succeed, even if you don't like that person. You will see wonders of improvement in your relationships.

One of my mentors, Chuck, would always challenge me to be a "There you are" person instead of a "Here I am" person. He would train us every time we walked into a room to say to ourselves, "There you are" to everyone in the room. We are naturally wired to want to impress others and be liked. This makes us unconsciously selfish. But if we change our mindset from being all about me to all about others and if we put others first and seek to understand them, then our actions will say, "There you are!"

Practice Gratitude

Gratitude is an essential part of our EQ that also deeply affects our relationships with others. Reflecting on our blessings and what we have has real power to affect our disposition and our mood. It can also influence how we treat others. If we only focus on what we don't have or what we haven't accomplished, we inevitably feel unhappy, dissatisfied, and even resentful toward others. We can never achieve everything to make us completely happy or fulfilled.[43]

For example, in the 1970s, John Paul Getty had amassed a fortune and was considered the richest man in the world, but it wasn't enough for him. Someone kidnapped his grandson, and he initially refused to pay any of the $17 million ransom set for his release. A crime thriller film released in 2017 called *All the Money in the World* centers around the kidnapping, and the following is a brief exchange portrayed in the film between Fletcher Chase, a former CIA operative trying to help with the grandson's release, and John Paul Getty:

> **Fletcher Chase:** They will do things to Paul that cannot be undone for any amount of money. We have to pay.
>
> **John Paul Getty:** Well, this simply isn't possible. My financial position has changed.
>
> **Fletcher Chase:** Really? I mean, thirty seconds ago, you said it was a good day. I mean, I'm not all that bright, but I can multiply as well as you. With oil up as much as it was this morning, you have amassed another fortune.
>
> **John Paul Getty:** Well, what if the embargo is lifted and oil were to crash? I'd be exposed. I have never been more vulnerable financially than I am right now.
>
> **Fletcher Chase:** Mr. Getty, with all due respect, nobody has ever been richer than you are at this moment.
>
> **John Paul Getty:** I have no money to spare.
>
> **Fletcher Chase:** What would it take? I mean, what would it take for you to feel secure?
>
> **John Paul Getty:** More.[44]

More? More! How could the richest man in the world possibly want more? Getty stonewalled his entire family for months, refusing to pay a dime, that is, until a newspaper received his grandson's severed ear, after which Getty negotiated the ransom down to $2.2 million, a tiny fraction of his fortune. What is truly fascinating is that his company, Getty Oil, no longer exists. It went bankrupt in 2011 from having sold off numerous parts of its business over the years.[45] Getty Oil went from one of the most successful companies in the world to nonexistent in fewer than fifty years. Getty was a man who could never be fully satisfied, and he lacked any semblance of gratitude. Ultimately, neither his hard work nor his stonewalling mattered. Everything that he spent his life working on and amassing disappeared. He left no legacy—just a trail of brokenness in his wake.

Gratitude helps us reflect and focus on the good in our lives. It protects us from destructive emotions, such as greed and envy. We can all get better at practicing gratitude and improving our EQ. For you, practicing gratitude could mean keeping a written journal and recording ten things you are thankful for every day. Maybe you could add this reflection to your morning routine from chapter 2. Whatever method works best for you, work toward cultivating a strong sense of gratitude.

Learn Your "Buttons"

"He sure knows how to get under my skin." "She knows just how to push my buttons." We all have these supposed buttons, as if we're computers or machines. We have triggers that set off reactions in us, but we can control those reactions, and we can change our buttons. Do you pause before you speak, act, or type an email? Are you reactive or proactive? Do you react emotionally, or do you respond intentionally and thoughtfully?

Here are some of my buttons: people wasting my time, people giving terrible customer service, people changing plans at the last minute, and people cutting in line. I have disproportionate negative reactions when these things occur. Sometimes, they're physiological: my heart starts to race, my body temperature rises, and I become so agitated that I'm unable to focus on anything else. I have imaginary conversations with these people, in which I explain their error in great detail. When people cut in line, I can't keep quiet. I usually say something like, "Excuse me, you probably didn't see it, but did you know there was a line? It begins back there." Then I aggressively gesture toward the back of the line.

But these buttons of mine don't actually exist, and neither do yours. The reality is that we allow people to control our emotions when we choose to react in the ways that we do. No one can make you feel a certain way *unless you let them.* We must get to a place where we are content with our own identities, and although others' actions can and will disappoint us, we can't let them enrage or devastate us. This is the starting point for EQ.[46] Learn what sets you off so that you can learn to temper your reactions accordingly.

Use the Platinum Rule

In order to improve your EQ and better understand others, you have to understand and appreciate that people feel and express love in different ways. Think of someone you know who cares about you. It might be a family member, an old friend, or a significant other. How do you know they care? How do they show you love? This is a window into your love language (and theirs). A love language is how you express and receive love. Most of us give love the same way we receive it, but that's not the case for everyone. For more on this, we recommend Gary Chapman's seminal work called *The Five Love Languages*. It has helped countless relationships.

Sometimes, we think we're communicating love to someone we deeply care about, but they don't pick up on it … at all. For example, I lived in Virginia Beach right after college, and I started dating this great girl named Lindsay. We had been dating for a couple of months, and my annual fundraiser banquet dinner was coming up. It was one of the busiest weeks of my year. The event was scheduled on a Thursday night and roughly three hundred people would be in attendance. We hoped to raise a good portion of our budget. On Tuesday night, I was working late in the office around 8 p.m. when I decided to do something special for Lindsay. I picked up her favorite coffee drink and delivered it to her at 9 p.m. I stayed for about fifteen minutes before having to go back to the office to continue preparing for the event.

As I went to leave, she stopped me and asked, "What? You're going already?" I was shocked. My top two love languages are gift-giving and words of affirmation. Lindsay's were quality time and physical touch. We spoke different languages. I thought that by bringing her favorite drink, I was showing her how special she was to me and how much I cared about her. What she heard was, "You're worth fifteen minutes of my time." Neither of us was right or wrong. We were simply wired to communicate differently.

We all know the golden rule: treat others the way you want to be treated. But the platinum rule is to treat others how *they* want to be treated. After all, they might want to be treated differently than how you want to be treated.

You Hold the Keys

You hold the keys to change. You are capable of improving your EQ but only if you are willing to do so. Are you willing to put in the work? To grow your EQ requires courage, persistence, and practice. I promise it's worth it. It will improve your work life and your personal life. I started this chapter with a story about how I almost ran my entire team of college volunteers (and myself) into the ground. After my team had forgiven me, I instituted a regular practice of evaluation. This was not just me evaluating my leaders but also them evaluating me.

One of the questions I would ask during our one-on-one meetings every semester was, "What are my blind spots?" This showed me what they were experiencing and feeling. Even after fifteen years of these practices, I'm still working on it. I have a long way to go, but I've come a long way as well. Start a conversation like this with someone you trust—someone who you know truly cares about you. Ask them what blind spots you have and then listen. Write their answers down without responding or defending yourself or justifying your actions. Take some time after your conversation and reflect on it to discern the truth of what they share. Each of these steps is part of the growth process.

20 TIPS TO GROW YOUR EMOTIONAL INTELLIGENCE

1. Take control of your emotional state. Three deep breaths in and three deep breaths out.
2. Use the 10:10:10 method popularized by Warren Buffett. Ask yourself how this will make you feel after ten minutes, ten months, and ten years.
3. Be curious about people, places, and things. Be observant.
4. Write down things you feel, do, and think while frustrated, upset, or overwhelmed to help you identify patterns.

5. Utilize active listening skills. Don't be interesting; be interested. Ask good questions and try to hear with empathy and understanding. (See the list at the end of this chapter for inspiration.)

6. Smile more.

7. Remind yourself that your human dignity and worth does not come from others.

8. Find mentors who are emotionally intelligent.

9. Learn to apologize. "Emotional intelligence helps you realize that apologizing doesn't always mean you're wrong. It does mean valuing your relationship more than your ego."[47]

10. Ask "why" a lot.

11. Move toward discomfort and growth, not away from it.

12. Examine your empathy. Do you feel compassion for others? If not, why?

13. Consider things from another perspective. For example, say a car is speeding down your street in front of your house. You're angry and shake your fist and yell at the couple as they tear around the corner. The next day, a man comes back to your house and humbly apologizes because his wife had fallen and hit her head, and she was unconscious. He was speeding because time was of the essence as he rushed her to the hospital.

14. Think before reacting. Become a "person of the pause."[48] Take your time when responding, especially when the subject is highly emotional. Learn the difference between reacting and responding. Choose to respond.

15. Regulate negative emotions. People with high EQ still feel the same negative emotions as everyone else, but they have learned to channel those negative emotions into motivation and choose their reactions.

16. When expressing difficult emotions, learn the XYZ technique: "I feel X when you do Y in situation Z."

17. Get feedback. Ask others for perspective. Most of us don't see ourselves clearly. Some of your friends may not see you clearly either, but at least a few of them do.

18. Pay attention to your body language and nonverbal cues. What is your posture? Are your arms crossed while your coworker shares a new idea? He or she might read that as defensive. Do you roll your eyes when you disagree with someone? Chances are they don't appreciate it. Be mindful of what you're saying without words.

19. Reflect on these questions: What are my emotional strengths? What are my weaknesses?

20. Practice, practice, practice.

BE A SIDNEY

The goal of EQ is to become emotionally mature. Emotional maturity is the application of EQ. Two hallmarks of emotional maturity are taking responsibility for your actions and remaining positive and optimistic.

First, when something goes wrong, do you step up and own the mistake, or do you search for an excuse? Winners take responsibility; losers blame others. One of my first mentors after college had a "fall on your sword" principle. He said that as soon as you realize you have made a mistake, you should immediately come clean and do your best to fix it. When you mess up, fess up. It's amazing how much grace people have for those who admit their mistakes. Life is about taking responsibility for your actions and your reactions.

Secondly, do you approach life with a positive spirit, or is everything always going wrong? We all know someone whose attitude is like Eeyore's from *Winnie-the-Pooh*. They are a Debbie Downer whose glass isn't even half empty. On the other hand, some people are positive, optimistic, and generally excited to be alive despite whatever their circumstances may be. We get to choose which type of person we will be.

Josh has the perfect example of someone who possessed emotional maturity in spades. Meet Sidney:

> Several years ago, when my wife and I took over as the owners of a Chick-fil-A in Little Rock, Arkansas, we met a young lady named Sidney. She was one of our first hires. She was fifteen years old at the time, and she was quickly working circles around the rest of the group. She lived with her grandmother, brother, and a couple of cousins. She was from a tougher part of town, and throughout her middle and high school years, she saw her peers—friends, neighbors, and relatives—become pregnant, get addicted to drugs, join gangs, or end up in jail.
>
> Despite her surroundings, Sidney continuously took ownership over her life and made decisions that no one in her life was making. She got a job before she could drive. She used her paychecks to help provide for her grandmother. She was an honor student in high school and was ultimately accepted into the University of Arkansas. Even in college it would have been easy to make poor decisions, but time and again Sidney pursued her vision of a better future and demonstrated emotional maturity. She didn't allow her environment to dictate her feelings, emotions, decisions, or reactions.
>
> Sidney graduated from college with incredible grades and was accepted into Texas A&M's law school. We are incredibly proud of what she has accomplished and continues to accomplish in her life. She is a perfect example of someone who was exceptionally emotionally mature for her age and developmental stage.

Why is it that some people grow up to become emotionally mature adults capable of cultivating healthy relationships, while others seem to remain socially incompetent? We've all seen celebrities—grown men and women—throw tantrums. It turns out that only 36 percent of adults are able to accurately identify their emotions as they happen.[49] This means that roughly two in three people are controlled by something they can't readily identify. This is scary, but we've all experienced both sides of this coin. We've reacted emotionally for reasons we can't quite explain, or we've been on the receiving end of a confusing emotional response. What makes emotional maturity so wonderful is that it costs no money and requires no formal education. Each and every one of us has the ability to grow in this area, and as we increase our emotional intelligence, we discover new opportunities to develop our emotional maturity as well.

It's always good to have a starting point, so we would like to offer you a fun, non-scientific test to gauge your emotional maturity level. This is not being recorded, there is no grade, and you will not be handing it in. Only one rule: answer honestly.

Emotional Maturity Survey

Mark 1 for all the time, 2 for sometimes, and 3 for rarely, then total your score at the end.

1. I take responsibility for my actions.
2. I recognize and admit when I am wrong.
3. I recognize that I am biased.
4. I can identify some of my biases.
5. I recognize and accept my own feelings and needs.
6. I never feel that I am a victim.
7. I can identify how people feel and how they are experiencing me.
8. I set healthy boundaries in my relationships.
9. I pause between feeling and reacting.
10. I showcase compassion for others.
11. I have the ability to get through challenging situations.
12. I have a positive outlook on life.
13. I live a life where my actions mostly line up with my words.
14. I possess self-control.

15. I think about others first.
16. I delay gratification.
17. I express gratitude.
18. I listen for the purpose of understanding.
19. I rarely take a mistake personally.[50]
20. I possess a mindset where I am open to learning and growing.[51]

0–19: Not possible. Use a calculator next time.

20: In the words of Buddy the Elf, "You sit on a throne of lies!" May we suggest rereading chapter 1: Know Yourself?

21–25: You attract healthy relationships, but are you certain that you are self-aware?

26–40: Most of us land in this zone.

41–50: Congratulations on being honest with yourself. This is a great place to be, and you know how to move forward.

51+: You are the Incredible Hulk and smash every relationship you are in.

Of course, you can tell that this quiz is in no way scientific but simply intended to make you laugh and think. It's a compilation of thoughts and behaviors to serve as prompts for self-reflection. Sometimes, bringing attention to these kinds of things provides greater awareness of strengths and weaknesses.

CULTURAL INTELLIGENCE

We almost always want variety from the food we eat,
but almost never from the people with whom we eat.
Mokokoma Mokhonoana, philosopher, social critic, and writer

The world has become smaller, and thanks to technology, we can see what's going on all around the globe. *Glocalization*, or making international products and organizations adaptable to different local cultures, is a new phenomenon that's here to stay. With this increased exposure and interaction throughout the world, cultural intelligence, CQ (cultural quotient) for short, has never been more important. It's critical for international business, but CQ's greatest importance might be domestic, as it's essential in personal and professional relationships with people who are different from you.

According to Randstad, a company and global leader in the human resources industry, "Cultural intelligence is more than just cultural awareness and sensitivity … it is the ability to relate to culturally diverse situations, as well as work effectively in them." That includes but is not limited to adaptability, empathy, and relational skills. CQ is a measure of a person's capacity for cross-cultural interaction and ability to function effectively with people and situations in cultures outside of their own. Furthermore, it "achieves better results … and allows a company to adapt quickly to different environments."[52]

One of my dear friends, Jael Chambers, is a national diversity expert. He founded a diversity consultant firm called Cultured Enuf and was gracious enough to share some thoughts on CQ:

> The U.S. Census Bureau reports that by the year 2050, racial minorities will make up the majority of the population. You may have already noticed this demographic shift in your school, hometown, place of worship, apartment complex, neighborhood, or other places. As we get closer and closer to 2050, the ability to interact effectively with diverse groups will become a requirement for almost every job you apply for. The measurement of this skill is called your cultural intelligence.
>
> Simply put, it's your aptitude for healthy and genuine interactions with others, especially people who are different from you. Your ability to notice and interpret human

behavior from gestures to idioms to food preferences is an important part of excelling in the workplace. It can also enhance your personal relationships, encounters with neighbors, travel experiences, and so much more.

Here are three practical suggestions from Jael to help boost your CQ:

Step 1: Become Aware of Your Own Culture

Take time to reflect on the culture you are a part of. How were you raised? What does your family value? How did your parents talk about people who look different? What do your actions say about your beliefs? How do you feel when conversations about race or ethnicity arise?

Step 2: Be Humble, Sit Down

A genuine posture of listening is essential for improving your CQ. Humility is key. Ask yourself these questions:

- What does my body language convey?
- Do I ask questions for clarity?
- Am I often defensive or feel the need to correct someone?
- Am I genuinely curious about the person I'm talking with?

Try this simple listening exercise: Ask someone to share their experience of high school, college, or work. Before entering the conversation, prepare yourself to have a posture of listening and reflection.

Step 3: Make Time

Ultimately, there is no shortcut for understanding someone different than you. You have to take initiative and make time to learn about another culture, which is the only way to authentically improve your CQ. Read books by authors of different races and ethnicities. Invite a colleague of a different background to lunch. Listen to a different style of music or watch a movie that centers around a culture other than yours. Spend time in a different neighborhood. The possibilities are endless.

I've seen my CQ grow through two other effective methods. One:

international travel. It's not cheap but go out and see the world if you can make it work with your budget. Travel experience has helped me learn through trial and error how to interact with people of different backgrounds. When you leave the boundaries of the US, try to explore and see parts of the country that might not be on the well-worn tourist path. Two: I've seen my CQ grow is genuine friendships with people of different ethnicity than me. As my friendships grow deeper, I've discovered how to listen and learn.

We all fall in different places on the spectrum of EQ, CQ, and emotional maturity. If you want to move forward, you have to know where to start. Hopefully, this chapter showed you some areas of strength as well as opportunities for growth. If you want to become an expert at cycling, you have to practice cycling. If you want to become an expert in finance, you need to study finance. The same is true if you want to become an emotionally healthy adult. It takes time and practice. Don't get discouraged. We're behind you, rooting for you and cheering you on.

BIG IDEA

You can develop your EQ and CQ. When you improve these types of intelligence, you also become more emotionally mature. Both qualities help you at work, at home, and in relationships. It's worth it, and the people in your life are worth it.

LEAD OTHERS

JOSH

Leading by force never works well. My wife, Katie, and I have learned this the hard way by parenting two toddlers. Something you need to know about our children is that they are the pickiest eaters to have ever walked this planet. We tried everything we could think of to encourage them to try new foods. We talked to their pediatrician, read parenting books, and let them play with their food—all with minimal success.

One unforgettable night, our family was sitting around the dinner table. Our daughter, Lyla, was four, and our son, Brody, was two. They liked cheese, and they liked bread, so I made grilled cheese sandwiches for them. And yet, my sandwiches were met with looks of disgust. Somehow, the thought of cheese melted on bread revolted them. We came to the end of the meal, and I told Lyla that I would not excuse her from the table until she tried a bite of her sandwich. I wasn't pushing her to try brussels sprouts, asparagus, or any of the foods usually deemed gross by kids. It was a grilled cheese sandwich! Lyla's meltdown ensued, and we entered a standoff.

Lyla crawled into Katie's lap, looking for an ally, but Katie encouraged Lyla to try it too. After extensive pleading and negotiation (I may have offered to pay for her college), she finally took a bite. We were thrilled. In went the bite of grilled cheese, and for a moment, we could see that she truly liked it. She gave a suppressed smile that she hoped we wouldn't see. However, Lyla had already decided that she would use her superpower and gag. She is the only child I have ever known who can gag on command, and she knowingly does it to gain control. It's a power move. Even though she liked the sandwich, her gag reflex was already in full swing. She started to gag and then looked at me as if to say "I told you" before throwing up all over herself, Katie, and the floor. Katie, who was pregnant at the time, immediately darted to the bathroom and proceeded to throw up herself.

There I stood in the middle of the kitchen with a crying four-year-old covered in vomit, a frustrated wife in the bathroom, and a two-year-old staring blankly at me. I took the kids to the bathtub, and Katie took a shower. It was clear that the mess was mine to clean. Fair enough.

Once I had fully bathed the kids, I ventured to the kitchen to finish cleaning up the mess. Katie's only request occupied my mind: don't let Brody run through the kitchen. I walked into the kitchen, turned to grab paper towels, and in a flash that would make your head spin, Brody sprinted through the vomit and proceeded to track it throughout the house. This parenting fail reminded me that leading by force is not the way to lead. People just don't respond well to it.

AUTHENTIC LEADERSHIP

Let me tell you about a different kind of leader: Darrell Wallraven. Darrell was one of the most authentic leaders I have ever known. He was in his late sixties and simply needed a job to keep him busy. He joined our team at Chick-fil-A, and we ended up working together for nearly four years.

When he first came to work for us, Darrell instantly gravitated toward the dining room, where he built relationships with our guests and other members of our team. But Darrell didn't just work in the dining room. He made our location a place where people wanted to be. He was always cracking jokes, giving someone a hard time, or having fun. He could have been content walking around, sweeping floors, and wiping tables, but he wasn't. He got to know guests and even recruited new people to work on our team.

Darrell never had direct reports, wasn't a leader by title, and never led a major area of our business, but he changed lives every time he went to work. Marriages have taken place because of Darrell's influence. Savings accounts have been created. Entire life trajectories have been altered, and at no point was he in charge of anyone. He knew he would have a greater impact by going beyond the job description.

Darrell tragically passed away after a very brief battle with cancer in 2018. The service held in honor of his life was overflowing with people grateful to have known him, including his Chick-fil-A family, both guests and team members. People shared the enormous impact left by this man. He cared more about loving those around him than any job title. As a result, he was one of the finest leaders I have ever had the privilege to work with.

If you're not a boss or in charge of others in some capacity, then you probably read the title of this chapter ("Lead Others") and wanted to skip it. But the reality is that if you are reading this book, then you are probably early in your career. Maybe you are in your first or second job. Maybe you just earned a promotion. You may not have a lot of direct reports, but that doesn't mean you can't be a leader. Before you dismiss this as one of those "everyone gets a trophy" chapters, hear me out.

I want you to abandon the idea of leadership as someone who is in charge of someone else. Can you lead without having followers? The answer is undoubtedly yes. Whether you realize it or not, you are leading something each and every day. It is easy to reject that statement as false, especially if you don't hold a formal title or position that signifies this responsibility, but you don't need it. Leadership is not about being in charge.

Comedian Brian Regan describes what he calls "the Me Monster," which is someone who is all about themselves. While someone is speaking, the Me Monster is thinking about what they are going to say to appear clever or witty. When someone else tells a story, the Me Monster waits to one up the storyteller with their own story to top it. Regan tells a story of how he had two wisdom teeth pulled, and a self-focused Me Monster jumped in and said, "That ain't nothing. I had all four pulled."

We all bend toward the selfish and self-obsessed Me Monster, but if we want to lead others effectively, we need to resist this tendency. Authentic leadership maximizes the potential of others through influence and impact. It serves others and dismisses our inner Me Monster. Kevin Kruse, author and serial entrepreneur, describes leadership as "a process of social influence, which maximizes the efforts of others, toward the achievement of a greater good."[53]

You can choose to lead at any time and in any place, not just at work. But before you lead someone, you have to lead something. Fortunately, each of us is already a leader over something. Even if you're working an entry-level position, you're leading that position. If Darrell had not taken ownership of his broom and done a remarkable job serving in the dining room, he would not have created the impact that he ultimately did.

If you google the word *leadership*, millions of results pop up. But I think we can summarize *who* an authentic leader is with just two qualities: a strong sense of integrity and a genuine concern for others. And you don't need a title to exemplify these qualities. They're must-haves, whether you're sixteen and working your first part-time gig or you're the CEO of a Fortune 500 company.

Another example of authentic leadership is Dan Cathy, the CEO of Chick-fil-A. Whenever Chick-fil-A opens a new restaurant, they throw a huge party. Over a hundred people often camp out overnight in the parking lot, a DJ plays music, and plenty of food is served. These grand opening events are wonderful opportunities for support staff from Atlanta to come out and engage with the owner/operator of the location as well as the community. I once had the privilege to attend one of these openings with Dan Cathy.

A week prior to a new location's opening date, I received a call from Dan's secretary. She asked if I would be interested in joining Dan on a trip to the New Orleans market to visit a few other local restaurants. I jumped at the chance. I flew to Atlanta so that I could fly to New Orleans with Dan and other Chick-fil-A staff. While we were in the air and preparing to land, he huddled up the small group of us and set forth the vision. Dan told us that our purpose in being there was to connect with and care for the operator, their team, and their community.

Next, Dan told the group that we were going to sleep in the parking lot with all of the guests until the store opened the next morning. I don't know about you, but I have never slept in the parking lot of a restaurant before. And I couldn't believe that Dan would, especially considering he could have slept comfortably at the fanciest hotel in town. Heck, Dan could have bought that fancy hotel. But he didn't. He popped open his little Coleman tent, which had the names of each location he had camped out at written in Sharpie marker. At the time, Dan was nearing his one-hundredth opening. And not only did Dan have his own tent, but he also packed and provided tents, sleeping bags, and pillows for each of us traveling with him.

What struck me throughout the entire experience was Dan's desire to serve those around him. Throughout the entire evening, Dan genuinely engaged with and cared for the new team and operator. I even saw him picking up trash in the parking lot. I don't know about you, but if I were a CEO worth millions of dollars, it would be hard for me to want to sleep outdoors on newly poured concrete in the Louisiana heat, surrounded by more than one hundred other people. But Dan is a unique leader. He demonstrates care for those around him and exhibits some of the strongest character of anyone I have ever met.

Strong character is foundational to great leadership. Nothing disintegrates a business or a relationship faster than a lack of integrity. Think about wildly successful businesses that have been led by people of less-than-stellar ethics. Firms such as Arthur Andersen, Enron, and Tyco come to mind. Each of these organizations' leaders knowingly engaged in fraudulent activity. Being a person whom others trust will propel you forward regardless of whether you are in charge. Then, when you finally land that job or that promotion you've been working toward, your strong character will serve as the foundation for everything else that you do.

BECOME AN AUTHENTIC LEADER

What does an authentic leader actually *do* in order to achieve success? It starts inside the mind. Even as a leader, you work for someone. Maybe you work in a traditional organizational structure with a hierarchy, or perhaps you work directly for the customers whom you serve. Ultimately, we all report to someone, and if we keep in mind whomever it is that we serve, then our minds are prepared to take greater leaps in developing the other qualities that authentic leaders exhibit. Authentic leaders take ownership, possess competence in their field, communicate effectively, have a high decency quotient, and improve continuously.

Take Ownership

Think of yourself as a stress deflector. You exist in your job to deflect stress from someone. Let's say it's the customer. You work to make their product or shopping experience quicker and better. Perhaps your job is to deflect stress from your boss by performing the tasks and responsibilities assigned to you.

Personally, I have worked with "leaders" who have only made my job as a business owner more challenging. I had to hold their hand constantly, or they vented all of their problems to me. These behaviors do not exhibit leadership to your boss. Instead, they demonstrate that you focus first and foremost on yourself when you're supposed to be focusing on handling the pressures of the people for whom you work.

If you have a boss, you want to show autonomy. Move from asking your boss what to do when you have a question to discovering the answer for yourself. Instead of waiting for your boss's validation when making a decision, make the decision and then notify your boss so that they're aware of it. Fewer words are sweeter to a boss's ears than *I took care of it.* Remember: you can lead tasks even if you don't lead people. And if you lead those tasks well, your opportunities to lead people will increase exponentially.

In order to properly deflect stress, you need to learn how to appropriately take ownership. Often, the most frustrating challenge is when no one takes responsibility for actions or results—they're always someone else's fault. This goes back to basic maturity, but you would be astonished at how many people are prepared to blame someone else whenever something fails to go according to plan. Is this something you do? Do you blame others for unfavorable situations you find yourself in? These are the trappings of a victim mentality, which you want to avoid. Instead, be the person who says, "I did that," and then move on. One of my favorite books is called *Extreme Ownership*, and I highly recommend it if you want more on this topic.

Possess Competency

Any respectable leader in an organization needs to exhibit competency in whatever roles and responsibilities he or she is asked to do. Competency is the baseline; mastery is the objective. In order to be a masterful employee or boss, you need to seek additional knowledge. Others will not respect you or entrust you with additional opportunities if you cannot perform the basics of your job. Have you ever worked for bosses who were in charge but didn't do their jobs well? They may have been incredibly nice and well-liked, but without basic competency, chances are that no one respected them.

To become competent in something new, utilize the ESRC model. I have heard it used around Chick-fil-A for years, and I personally use it frequently for its impactful filter for leading:

- Expectations. Ask yourself what it is that you are expected to do. Be sure you clearly understand what your role is and define success with the person to whom you report.
- Skills. What skills do you need to learn? Talk to people who have already mastered the skills you want to develop.
- Resources. What resources are required to execute the job effectively? Ensure that you have the proper amount of time,

training materials, technology, and whatever else you may need to execute the expectations.

- Consequences. If you wield the other three elements, then both positive and negative consequences are entirely in your court.

Communicate Clearly

Being an authentic leader requires effective communication skills. That doesn't mean that others expect you to deliver inspiring, moving speeches every time you open your mouth. But it does mean that you want to participate in challenging conversations, ask insightful questions, showcase emotional maturity, engage with and develop others, and cope with disappointment in a healthy way.

All of us will face struggles throughout our careers, guaranteed. How will we deal with them? When a situation arises that you need to address, how will you respond? Will you ignore it? Make passive-aggressive remarks? Gossip about it with others? How will you approach challenges in a healthy and professional manner?

Leaders are sometimes required to have tough conversations. Author Tim Elmore uses the analogy of a velvet-covered brick. You have to have the tough conversation (the brick), but you want to do it with kindness and grace (the velvet). Do you favor truth or grace? Knowing yourself and your communication style can help you establish balance. Here are a few other tips and tricks to help you have those difficult discussions:

- Be sure you've already established a bridge of relationship with the other person before you bring truth over it.
- Talk about the issue, not the person.
- Keep the conversation concise, timely, and on topic.
- Don't engage with high emotions or loud voices.
- Come from a place of wanting to help, not calling someone out.

The ability to ask insightful, impactful questions is another critical skill set for any communicator. Do you know how to ask great questions that advance the dialogue? Nothing is more frustrating than what I call "parent questions." These are questions that parents tend to ask kids, and these questions only leave room for simple answers, such as yes and no. Questions like, "Did you have a good day at school? Are you worried about the test? Did you have fun?" These questions are poor because they do not elicit meaningful conversation. Productivity guru Michael Hyatt published a blog post about asking more powerful questions. Here are the highlights:

1. "Ask open-ended questions." Unlike the examples above, ask questions that lead to more than one-word answers.
2. "Get behind the assumptions." Ask questions that help you understand the other person's assumptions.
3. "Get both sides of the story." I have messed this one up a ton. I get half the information and then act on it, only to learn later that I didn't have the full story.
4. "Ask follow up questions." Try to ask "why" to continue digging deeper into the answer.
5. "Get comfortable with 'dead air.'" It's completely acceptable to be quiet while waiting for a response. You wouldn't believe what people say when they become uncomfortable with quiet.
6. "Help people discover their own insights." When people discover for themselves, they learn much more than when they are told. You don't have to say the answer. Try to lead those with whom you are talking to the correct conclusion. They will remember far more from that.
7. "Understand the difference between facts and speculation." Ask questions that get to the core of the truth and not an interpretation of it.[54]

Possess and Promote DQ

No, DQ in this instance does not stand for Dairy Queen, although their Blizzards are delicious. DQ stands for decency quotient, or decency intelligence. The word *decency* was six times more likely to appear in books written in English in 1800 than it is today.[55] Decency is not a sexy topic that the latest webinar or TedTalk is likely to address, so what does this obscure fact have to do with our everyday life? According to Peter Tufano, Dean of Oxford Saïd Business School, "The concept of decency remains relevant—even necessary—in today's world of brashness and social media self-indulgence."[56]

Whereas people commonly understand IQ and EQ, fewer are aware of DQ, and even fewer possess it. Bill Boulding, Dean of Duke University's Fuqua School of Business, would agree with Tufano, as Boulding says that many business leaders lack this critical factor. According to Boulding, "EQ doesn't mean a person's actions take into account what is best for others. Emotional awareness and empathy don't equate to compassion and integrity. People can have EQ yet use it to manipulate people for self-interest ... DQ means wanting something positive for everyone in the workplace and ensuring everyone feels respected and valued."[57]

Have you ever seen the Geico Gecko? One of Pete's dearest friends' dad, Dean, worked hard to make that campaign famous, and I think it's safe to say he succeeded. Here are a few words from Pete on Dean:

> Dean was the most positive person I've ever known. He possessed a raw, unbridled optimism that was a force to be reckoned with. It was almost as if his "look on the bright side" attitude was written into his DNA. One time, out of the blue, he sent me a personalized, home video of him rapping birthday wishes for me. Tragically, Dean became sick with degenerative brain cancer, and as it progressed, his optimistic attitude overrode any desire he might have had to complain or entertain negativity. In light of his cancer diagnosis, he made it a point to tell his loved ones that he cared about them more than ever.
>
> I fight negativity when the elevator in my building takes too long or when someone cuts me off in traffic, but Dean's DQ was off the charts. Unsurprisingly, his wife, MK,

his son, Will, and his daughter, Cate, also all have DQ in spades. Dean lived others-focused and was an example of a life well-lived. His DQ is an example for us all.

You, too, can promote decency in your personal life and in your organization.[58] Start by considering yourself promoted to CEO no matter what your current job title is. You are now the brand-new Chief Encouragement Officer of your workplace. Catch others doing good and tell other people about it. Be a "there you are" type of person. Pick one person per day and encourage him or her intentionally. This can also be accomplished by asking coworkers how they are doing, not only in their work lives but also as individuals. Thank others and fully appreciate what they do and who they are. Have an eye to recognize those who are underrepresented or have difficulty voicing their opinion, and help amplify their voice. Give away your power and privilege. Examine your words and actions toward others. Are you pausing and trying to see their perspective?

Whatever your context or position may be, create a culture in which feedback is celebrated as a mechanism to help everyone grow in pursuit of the mission, not just as a tool for criticism. You can do this by providing frequent opportunities for communication and dialogue. Give timely feedback, coaching, and training for anyone you supervise. It is essential to lead others in your workplace toward win-win situations. At all costs, avoid the "zero-sum" philosophy. This philosophy promotes the idea that one person's gain necessitates another person's loss, meaning someone wins and someone loses in every situation. Instead, brainstorm situations where everyone can win. In many workplaces, different departments remain separated or even compete with each other. This kind of setup creates silos. Resist the silos! Be the first to reach your hand over every divide and work as a team. Even if someone makes you angry, avoid the temptation to burn bridges. Never send an email or a text or make a phone call when you are angry. Wait.

Most of all, be considerate and kind. Kindness is underrated. Be unselfish not only of the spaces you share but also in the lives of others—at home, at work, and in public. If your roommate or spouse takes out the trash, take initiative by taking it out the next time it's full. If Stacy from accounting mentions her daughter's dance recital is coming up this weekend, write a note on your phone to ask her how it went the following Monday. Don't take calls on speaker phone in the grocery store. Or in any store. Or in any public place for that matter.

You reap what you sow. It's an old adage, but we can trust it as one of the many laws of the universe. Plant positivity and reap positivity. It may take a long time before you can harvest, and sometimes we don't even see the results. Over one thousand people attended Dean's funeral. He sowed seeds of decency throughout his life, put others first, and left a tremendous impact on this world. That's what a legacy is. Choose kindness and be decent. Be positive. It's contagious.

Continuously Improve

The smartest people I know are constantly learning. They understand that there is so much they *don't* know. This understanding and awareness drives them forward to continuously expand their minds. The people who think they have everything figured out are often the most ignorant. If you are not constantly seeking to learn and grow, then you will be left behind—and quickly.

Sometimes, we think there is only one way to learn, but this couldn't be further from the truth. When I think about personal development in my life, my biggest strides have always been a product of an experience that was outside of my comfort zone and required me to step up. As a result, I try to do something every year that is completely uncomfortable for me. For example, one year I attended a seminar on public speaking, one of my least favorite activities.

Another year, I wrote a book, which ultimately became *Adulting 101*. And another year, I became a dad. Nothing pushes you to grow quite like parenthood. If you stop and reflect for a moment about the times in your life during which you grew the most, perhaps they, too, were driven by experience. Sign up for new experiences that fall outside your comfort zone, travel, listen to podcasts on subjects that interest you, listen to audiobooks, and engage with other people in your industry.

Continuous improvement is a necessary habit for every leader. Whether you lead people or tasks, you must continually consider how to get better. Complacency will lead to the demise of your leadership, your job, or your company.

AUTHENTIC LEADERSHIP MATTERS

Authentic leaders like the incredible aforementioned Darrell Wallraven don't exist for a title or to earn more money. Oftentimes, they maximize their opportunities through impact and influence. Leading a life dedicated to providing a positive influence on the lives of others will quickly set you apart, whether you are in your first part-time job or the career from which you will retire. People will recognize a genuine, sincere care for others.

As I mentioned, Darrell didn't receive a promotion. He wasn't in it for recognition. He simply wanted to impact lives each day that he walked into the restaurant. You may not be in the job that will eventually become your career, but every job you have helps to prepare you for what is next. Just because something doesn't appear to be your career doesn't mean that you can't learn from the experience and apply the skills you acquire to become an even better candidate the next time.

BIG IDEA

You don't have to have a title or formal position to be an authentic leader. Utilize where you are and what you are doing and maximize that experience by having a positive impact on those around you. Seek to become an authentic leader regardless of where you are in your leadership journey.

5

SCREENS AND YOU

PETE

Think back to where you were and what you were doing just five years ago. Has the pace of life felt like it's accelerated since then? Kind of like an out-of-control, runaway truck? It seems like every year, the speed limit of our daily lives increases. So many things change, but one thing remains constant: life moves fast. Technology has been the engine for this frantic ramping up of everyday life, and the resulting amount of noise and distraction has become overwhelming without offering any real respite.

Are you able to be fully present wherever you are? Me neither. How many alerts or notifications have you received in the last ten minutes? Have you ever grabbed your phone to do something on it and then ten minutes (or two hours) later that you forgot your reason for picking it up in the first place? You might even be reading this book on your phone …

Josh has the perfect story of a time when his sister could not bring herself to be present during a family vacation:

> My wife, Katie, and I went on vacation in Costa Rica with my parents, my brother, his wife, and my younger sister. A spider the size of my hand crawled over my foot while I made pancakes (and yes, I have photographic evidence), but one of my main memories of the trip is the image of my college-aged sister curled up in a ball with her phone. It was connected to what must be the longest charging cord available for sale to the public. This thing must have been 200 feet long. At one point, I believe the charger was plugged in downstairs while

she sat upstairs in the living room. She could move anywhere in the house without unplugging her phone.

This cord was her lifeline, and I joked that it was her umbilical cord. She had so much activity on her phone that it was a necessity to her. I've never seen anyone type so fast or so furiously. There we were in one of the most beautiful places on the planet (with some of the biggest spiders), and my sister couldn't resist her screen.

Can you relate? Have you ever been somewhere and you or someone you were with couldn't put down their phone?

THE SCREEN EPIDEMIC

The current explosion of digital technology not only is changing the way we live and communicate but is rapidly and profoundly altering our brains.
Gary Small, UCLA professor of psychiatry [59]

YouTube is the second-most-visited site after Google. Two billion users log in to YouTube every month. YouTubers upload five hundred hours of new content every minute, and viewers watch over five billion videos every day. This equates to over eighty-two years of new video daily, which is more than the programming total of the first twenty years of TV! It is difficult to comprehend the amount of time that we spend watching videos.

The average adult in America spends more than eleven hours per day looking at some type of screen: a computer, TV, phone, or tablet. For those who rely on computers for their work, this amount of screen time is somewhat unavoidable, but they're still consuming a considerable amount after work hours. How are our new tech and screen habits affecting us? It's too soon to draw any substantial conclusions about long-term effects because it's a relatively new phenomenon. We don't truly know just yet, but the initial research is disturbing. We know that over two-thirds of car accidents are caused by distracted drivers—many of whom are looking at their phones. Excessive screen time can lead to numerous health concerns, including eye strain, headaches, insomnia, sleep disruption, tendonitis, and other injuries, not to mention the risks associated with leading a sedentary lifestyle, which has been linked to heart disease, obesity, and other health problems.[60]

According to Nicholas Carr, author of *The Shallows: What the Internet Is Doing to Our Brains*, "When we go online, we enter an environment that promotes cursory reading, hurried and distracted thinking, and superficial learning. Even as the Internet grants us easy access to vast amounts of information, it is turning us into shallower thinkers, literally changing the structure of our brain."[61] The existence of a constant stream of new content that we continually consume during any free moment in our day has alienated the already challenging practices of reflection and deep thinking, banishing them to almost nonexistence. Sometimes I wonder if computers are programming us instead of us programming computers.

Alienation … is an inevitable by-product of the use of technology.
Nicholas Carr[62]

LIVING WITH TECHNOLOGY

Whether or not we realize it, technology can have a monumental impact on who we are, how we perceive ourselves, and even the development of our brains. Take Tia for example.

Tia's Story

Tia was a sophomore in college and extremely social. Her social circles knew her for her bubbly personality and social media savvy. She didn't have a job and was not in school on a scholarship. Her parents provided her a small monthly stipend and paid her cell phone bill. After a semester of vigorous partying, Tia's grades began to drop, and she was placed on academic probation. When her parents discovered that her grades had dropped significantly, they cut her off financially and took away all of her devices, including her phone, tablet, and personal computer. Her parents told her she would have to use the phones in the dorm room for calls and the local computer lab for all school assignments. Tia was devastated.

She was too embarrassed to tell her friends what had happened or use the school computer lab for social media, and the thought of borrowing an old cell phone from a friend humiliated her. She became extremely anxious about the social events and life stories she was missing out on. In fact, Tia was so upset that she threatened to kill herself if her parents did not return her devices. Her parents were so worried about her safety that they called the local mental health crisis mobile team and had Tia psychologically evaluated and admitted to a treatment facility. Her reaction to the loss of her devices may seem extreme, but her emotional attachment to her devices is not that difficult to explain or relate to.

Like many young adults, Tia spent most of her time interacting with technology, watching Netflix, and scrolling through social media. She would regularly check her phone for texts, posts, gatherings, and gossip. The precise moment is not clear, but at some point, Tia began to associate her identity and self-worth with others' perceptions of her. The "views" and "likes" on social media apps gave her feelings of validation, belonging, and instant gratification. Her parents had no idea they were also taking away those feelings when they took away her devices. Because the internet operates at such a high speed, gratification is often instant. To a developing brain, this can be powerfully addictive. After Tia returned to school, she sought a counselor to help her identify and understand her emotions, determine the origins of her wants and desires, and find healthy, sustainable ways to connect with others. The counselor also helped Tia develop a stronger sense of self-worth and a positive self-image.

The vast number of technology options, the breadth and magnitude of the internet, as well as the speed at which we process information contributes to something called *cognitive load*. Cognitive load is basically our brain's capacity for how much information it can handle at once. When the load becomes too much, it impairs our memory, connections, and aptitude for conceptualizing. Our basic ability to learn becomes impaired. This is scientific jargon for "it makes us dumber," and it's what happens while we surf the internet or refresh our social media feeds.

Screen use not only decreases our memory and learning, but it can also affect how we feel. A 2016 study of over forty thousand young people showed that beyond one hour of use, additional hours of daily screen time were associated with lower psychological well-being.[63] This includes less curiosity, lower self-control, more distractibility, more difficulty making friends, less emotional stability, and inability to finish tasks. This is daunting information. The study furthers shows that people with extremely high screen use were more than twice as likely to receive a diagnosis of depression and/or anxiety, to receive treatment from a mental health professional, or to take mental health medication. Yikes. Other studies suggest similar findings. At the end of the day, we know that screens and technology, when used excessively, are harmful to our health.

VIDEO GAMES

When I moved to Harrisonburg, I met one of the most interesting people in the world. His name was Nathan. He was a hip-hop genius who looked more like a punk rock hipster. After Nathan graduated college, he continued living in a college house. He landed a great job with James Madison University researching a cure for deafness and worked with bird cochleae. Humans also have cochleae, which are organs inside our ears that allow us to hear. I didn't even know birds had cochleae. Nathan also introduced me to the mixed martial arts sports competition called Ultimate Fighting Championship (UFC). He once tried to show me what had happened during a fight by tapping me on the head and saying, "Go to sleep." But he missed the top of my head and instead tapped me square on my nose, which I had recently broken. The mere tapping of the bridge of my nose brought me to my knees in pain. That's the type of friend Nathan was.

Nathan started to earn a decent wage but continued to live in a super cheap college house paying only $175 a month in rent. His bedroom slowly evolved into an extravagant man cave—complete with the latest electronics, music system, a huge TV, and all the latest video games and their apparatuses. But this season would not prove to be his best. He started playing video games all day every day and even competed in national tournaments against some of the best gamers in the world. Ironically, the thing he enjoyed most ended up hurting him physically. He developed crippling tendonitis in his hands from gaming, and the video games took over his life. It's tech or your life. And we only have one life to live, unlike Super Mario.

Video games are alluring because they are engineered to be addictive. They provide unique experiences that we can't replicate in other mediums. They're also convenient; nearly everyone can play *Call of Duty*, *Smash Bros*, or *Fortnite*. Another appealing aspect is the fantasy element. Video games contain a level of drama, excitement, and heartbreak that allow the user to experience a dramatic, first-person adventure. They allow us to enter another world, roleplay, and participate in a narrative that isn't otherwise available to us. They provide alternative methods for developing skills such as problem solving, creativity, and collaboration (assuming the game is multiplayer). Players can connect with each other all over the world, creating a sense of global community.

Real Jack has to pay bills, check his bank account regularly, and pay taxes. Video game Jack just slayed a dragon, completed a mission, and saved the world.
Jack, a twenty-something

A popular PlayStation ad promises that "greatness awaits." Unfortunately, this is a bald-faced lie. Escape to this imaginary world, press some buttons, and you will accomplish valiant, courageous feats. In this imaginary world, you have unlimited lives and countless opportunities to do the thing and get it right. Hit reset and start over as many times as you like. Unfortunately, these promises do not translate into the real world. Destructive choices have real consequences. You have to navigate difficult situations, and you often only get one shot. You can only accomplish greatness in the real world with real people.

We're not saying you should avoid video games altogether. What we are saying is that they are a recreational activity to be treated as such and enjoyed responsibly. It is responsible when you control the experience and the experience doesn't control you. If you have more *Fortnite* friends than in-person friends, you have a problem. It can be dangerous to limit your closest relationships to the virtual world. Beware the dangers of a sedentary lifestyle, a lack of social engagement, or increased aggression or violence. These are indicators of an unhealthy relationship with gaming. If your emotional and physical health or relationships are suffering, then gaming has become too great of a priority. Video games should complement your life, not dictate it.

One of our gamer friends has a rule that for every hour you spend playing video games, you have to do something creative, go outside, socialize, work out, or engage in real-world problem solving, be it a puzzle, volunteering, or an intellectual discussion with a friend. Figure out how you can use video games to bring people together, face-to-face, instead of isolating yourself in a room. Invite people over and play a game that is accessible to everyone. This balance is especially important if you've moved to a new place or started a new job. It can be all too easy to stay inside and game to avoid going out and meeting new people. If gaming is a routine part of your recreation, be careful to take care of your hands. Video games, computers, and cell phones induce an incredible amount of wear and tear on your hands that can lead to injuries down the road.

HEALTHY SCREEN TIME

Now let's talk about ways to practice healthy screen use in a more general sense. For starters, take a five-minute break every forty-five minutes while working in front of a screen. Even better is to walk and stretch during that break. When not at work, balance every hour of screen time with one hour of face-to-face interaction or one hour of creativity: write, draw, sing, play an instrument, paint, or knit. Avoid eating in front of a screen. This one's tough, at least for me, but studies have shown that people eat more when eating in front of a screen.[64] Don't charge your phone in your bedroom (use an old-fashioned alarm clock) and don't look at it for the first or last hour of each day. Why? The blue light that it emits prevents your brain from releasing melatonin, which makes you feel sleepy. If you absolutely must check your phone or watch a movie at night, wear blue light reducing glasses. They're affordable, and they actually work! I own a pair myself, and they're 100 percent worth the taunting from friends.

The tips in the last paragraph are actionable, concrete steps that you can take to set boundaries in your relationship with technology. Now let's think about your relationship as a whole. Specifically, think about your screen use and take an inventory. When using technology, ask yourself this: Is this technology serving me, or am I serving this technology? We must resist the hypnotic belief that satisfaction only comes through unceasing, frenetic activity. Indiscriminate, excessive tech use is harmful to our minds and bodies, but thoughtful, conscientious use can help us accomplish our goals and connect with others.

SCREENS AND EMOTIONAL INTELLIGENCE

The iPhone has a built-in feature called Screen Time, and it tracks your average weekly screen time in hours. It's one of the most convicting, embarrassing, and exposing features. I sometimes shake my head and say, "There's no way!" Occasionally, I consider disabling it altogether so that no one sees the actual amount of time that I spend "social networking," which is really just a nice way of saying "mindlessly scrolling through other people's photos."

Many of us use technology extensively in our daily jobs. I am certainly dependent on my technology. But we must differentiate between dependent and addicted. Currently, "83% of today's workforce considers email 'critical' to their success and productivity."[65] Email is still rated higher than the phone, conference calls, and texting. A big part of how we deal with tech will be learning to communicate effectively and clearly using written text—whether through email, text, or other workplace communications tools such as Slack. We have all received (and have probably sent) a scathing email or passive-aggressive text. Be mindful of your *netiquette*, your "etiquette on the net" or your style of interacting with people electronically. Below are guidelines for practicing emotionally intelligent electronic communication, which is particularly important in the workplace:

1. Communicate face-to-face or over the phone whenever possible. This gives you more freedom to express tone and avoid potential miscommunication and misinterpretation.

2. Never respond out of emotion. Abraham Lincoln accumulated piles and piles of scathing letters that destroyed his rivals, but he never sent them. He would write an emotional letter, stuff it in a drawer, return to it after a day or two, and write a more conciliatory letter. Write that wild-eyed email but don't press send. Sleep on it, come back to it the next day (or perhaps even two days later), and write a level-headed response.

3. Be extremely careful with humor, especially sarcasm and satire. While these make sense to the sender, the receiver has limited access to the tone in which it was sent and no access to body language, facial expressions, or voice inflections to aid their reading experience.

4. Remember that you are communicating with a person. Ask yourself if what you're typing is something you would say in person and to a person. It's easy to puff up with emotion and treat people more poorly than you would if you were looking them in the eye.

5. Electronic = forever. What you post, comment, or email forever exists in the digital world. For that reason, "Write praise and encouragement in stone and criticism in the sand." It's a good rule of thumb to write encouragement or positive communication in email and electronic format and save critical or tough communication for a phone call or face-to-face conversation. Afterward, next steps can be shared over email.

6. Some online chats need to move offline and become in person. It's tough to discern when an email thread or text conversation

becomes too heated or difficult to continue. When in doubt, finish it in person or over the phone.

7. Include a short, direct subject line in every email you send. This honors the time of the recipient and allows them to quickly discern the purpose of your email.

8. Only include necessary information and do not "reply all" when your message is not pertinent to all. An email that only reads "Thanks so much" needlessly clutters inboxes. Save yourself the time and show others that you respect theirs.

9. Avoid using ALL CAPS and unnecessary exclamation marks! I once received an email that was seven sentences long, and every sentence ended with an exclamation mark! When you attempt to emphasize everything, you emphasize nothing! Not only is it obnoxious, but it also reads as if you're yelling! If this short paragraph began to annoy you with its excessive use of exclamation marks, imagine receiving an entire email like this!

10. Follow your boss's lead. Allow management to set the tone for communication. Are emoticons/emojis permissible? How are they crafting their emails? Is it okay to include personal information?

11. Use the common consumption test. Would you want this email to be made public? Would it be appropriate for others to read? One wrong click is enough to send an email to the wrong person or people.

12. Reread or regret. "No regerts!" Read through your email at least once before sending it to avoid embarrassing errors.

13. Respond to emails within the accepted time frame guidelines of your workplace. Texts do not necessarily carry the expectation of a reply, but emails do. You can and should expect replies to emails. If you need a response within forty-eight hours, you must call or text. Email is not to be used for same-day plans or time-sensitive communication. If you do send a time-sensitive email, call, or text to let the recipient know it's urgent.[66]

SHHHH

Without great solitude, no serious work is possible.
Pablo Picasso (1881–1973), Spanish artist

Science has taught us that the busier we are, the more we need quiet time and reflection. How busy do you feel? How overwhelmed do you feel? The busier you are, the more you need silence.[67] We need figurative noise-canceling headphones to achieve clarity, but there are tangible ways of doing this. For example, the world-renowned Mayo Clinic encourages meditation as a practice to reduce stress.[68]

In fact, silence and meditation are surprisingly common practices among the world's top performers. At least 90 percent of the world's highest achievers in Tim Ferriss' book *Tools of Titans* mentioned reflection, meditation, and silence as important elements to their focus and success. Almost every single world champion, expert, innovator, and distinguished professional used meditation as part of their daily practice. What's more is that they attributed much of their success to this practice and said they couldn't live without it. Many said that the faster life sped up, the more necessary it became for them to pull away and reflect.[69] I've observed this to be true in my personal journey too.

I wish I had discovered the importance of silence and solitude much earlier in life, and I encourage you to experiment with it. Start with just a couple minutes of silence. Then slowly build up to greater lengths of time, and make it part of your daily routine. These periods of silence are your noise-canceling headphones to help you focus and clarify your mission. Technology is here to stay. We aren't trying to learn how to live *without* technology. We are simply learning how best to live *with* it.

BIG IDEA

Technology has undeniably changed us and will continue to do so. It is not evil in and of itself, but it will numb our souls if we let it, and it can become an evil depending on how we use it and how often. That's why it's all the more important that we set and maintain clear boundaries in our relationship with technology. And if you find yourself mindlessly scrolling (like I do), maybe it's time to see other people—literally.

6

SOCIAL MEDIA: A TROJAN HORSE

PETE

It was the summer of 2004, and my friend Andy and I were working four consecutive weeks at a camp in New York. Each week, about five hundred high schoolers visited, and our job was entertainment—the funny stuff. We, of course, had to include a "Games of Troy" event, as the epic film *Troy* starring Brad Pitt and Orlando Bloom had released earlier that year, and it was all the rage.

First, we asked Sean, one of the maintenance guys known for being an incredible woodworker, to build a Trojan horse big enough for both Andy and me to crawl inside. Sean outdid himself. When it was done, this majestic wooden Trojan horse stood nine feet tall. Only one catch: we had to lie on top of each other in a tight space in order to be hidden inside the body of it.

All five hundred campers would be led into the big meeting room right after breakfast. After some quick entertainment by others, Andy and I would come out to "sell" the all-camp Games of Troy competition. In full Trojan armor (constructed from plastic), we would cram into the horse's belly of darkness and wait backstage. We never knew exactly when the campers would finish, so we were sometimes left in there spooning each other for a while. It was thoroughly unpleasant. When it was showtime, someone would knock loudly on the door of the big meeting room. A friend who was in on our act would answer the door and wheel our giant horse inside. We had wireless microphones inside the horse and whispered to each other, pretending to be Greek warriors who had tricked the camp into letting us enter. Then we would burst out of the horse and declare the camp Troy, and the games would begin.

But during the last week of camp, someone pranked us. They soaked rags in deer repellent and left them in the body of the horse overnight. I don't know if you've ever smelled deer repellent, but it has to be one of the top ten worst smells on earth. When Andy and I tried to climb inside the Trojan horse the next morning, it proved nearly impossible. Those rags had stewed inside the body of the horse all night, and *pungent* doesn't even begin to describe it. The odor was violently rancid. Painfully and reluctantly, we crammed inside and proceeded to wait ten minutes before entering the room. It was the longest ten minutes of my life and felt like an eternity. Lying on top of each other, we couldn't stop from dry heaving. When they finally opened the horse, we stumbled out, nauseous and disheveled, looking as though we had already been through a battle instead of taking the stage by storm. The prank was one of the best ever. Or maybe the worst.

Here is the extent of my historical knowledge of the Trojan horse (supplemented by the internet, of course). The Trojan horse was a sneaky act of war. Around 1200 BC, the Greeks attempted to conquer the independent city of Troy, but after ten years of unrest and without having made progress, the Greeks pretended to withdraw from the city altogether. They sailed away, leaving a large wooden horse behind as an offering to Athena, the Greek goddess of wisdom. What the Trojans did *not* know was that the horse was hollow and secretly housed Greek warriors. The horse was brought into the city, and then at night, the Greeks snuck out of the horse's belly and opened the gate to the city so that other Greek warriors could help lay siege to it. The combined Greek forces flooded the city's streets, overrunning Troy and burning it to the ground. Social media is our personal Trojan horse.

SOCIAL MEDIA INVASION

During the COVID-19 pandemic, people naturally expected social media use to increase—just not as much as it did. In March 2020, at the beginning of the COVID-19 pandemic, TikTok became the most downloaded non-gaming app—in the world.[70] Many social media platforms reported surges in use between 30 and 40 percent. Some even doubled.[71] This information is telling. It's clear that we run to these apps when we're idling, killing time, or in need of a jolt of amusement. The Trojan horse was not what it seemed, and neither is social media.

Social media is an insatiable, hungry wolf. Its appetite is never satisfied because it eats up as much time as we're willing to give it, and then it wants more. Not only does it want more, but it continually *feeds* us more, often without our request. You see, many social media platforms feature an infinite loop of new content that constantly refreshes itself. Think of Instagram's "Explore," TikTok's "For You," or your Facebook feed. You can always find new content, usually uninvited.

In the last chapter, we covered our inundation of technology, specifically screens. Accompanying this mountain of new technology is the avalanche of social media. And as we previously discussed, we still lack a complete understanding of the impact of technology despite the countless books and articles published on these very topics. It's all too new. And while many of us have grown up with social media, it, too, is relatively new. Instagram released in October 2010, and Snapchat released less than a year later in July of 2011. And from there, it took a while for them to launch into the prolific, addictive apps that they've become. So while we don't yet know the long-term effects, we know that they're mostly negative, and we know that we have a problem. It's not all bad. But it's mostly bad.

Maybe you've heard the phrase "Trojan horse" used in other contexts. It represents subversion from the outside or anything that gains entry and access for nefarious or sabotaging purposes. In computers, a Trojan horse is any code that misleads its users of its true intent. Instead, it damages or disrupts a computer's programming. This is especially true of social media. It misleads us about its true intentions and disrupts our healthy programming. It sabotages our goals. It sabotages our hearts. It sabotages our lives. Like the Beastie Boys said, "Listen up y'all, it's a sabotage."

Social media claims to promote connection but actually breeds isolation. Social media claims to foster community but actually breeds division. Social media claims to boost happiness but actually breeds anxiety and depression. Social media claims to nurture relationships but actually breeds loneliness. Social media claims to offer freedom of individual expression but actually breeds comparison. Social media claims to provide information but actually breeds misinformation. Social media claims to advocate diverse perspectives but actually breeds silo thinking.

Social media claims to help focus but actually breeds distraction.

It's so sneaky. We've allowed this Trojan horse into the deepest places in our hearts. Social media has invaded our spaces and our lives to degrees that we never thought possible.

All the unhappiness of man arises from the single fact that they cannot stay quietly in their room, so they turn to diversions to distract themselves.
Blaise Pascal[72] (1623–1662), French theologian and philosopher

When I watch TikTok videos late at night, I don't consciously think, *I value watching this stranger do a silly dance more than I value my family, my friends, or my health.* When I lie in bed, scrolling through Instagram instead of sleeping, I don't consciously think, *Look at these pictures of mostly strangers doing cool stuff! This is way more important than my own rest or taking care of my body.* When I wake up in the morning and start scrolling through Twitter, I don't consciously think, *This celebrity's opinion of the latest* Bachelor *episode is more important than my goals for today.* It's the sneaky Trojan horse that we invited into the inner courtyard of our lives, where it has the power to dismantle and destroy from the inside out.[73]

Technology claims to offer better, clearer means of communication, but does it really? Often what we end up communicating is not what's actually happening. For example, I bet that you've lied using technology today. I know I did. Did you type "lol" or "hahaha" or "I'm dead" or use an emoji of someone laughing uncontrollably? Did you actually laugh out loud? Did you laugh so hard that you cried? Neither did I. I went through my texts and counted the number of times I typed "lol" or used a laughing emoji in one day and counted nineteen times. No audible laughs ever took place.

Social media has made it more difficult for us to form deep, meaningful relationships.[74] We have gotten used to interacting with a large number of our friends in mostly digital formats. How many "friends" do you have on Facebook without knowing who they actually are? How many people do you follow or who follow you on Instagram without ever having met in person? Facebook limits the maximum number of friends to five thousand, while social science experts would put the number of possible friends between 50 and 150.[75] And science would say we can only realistically have five to ten close friends at any given time.[76] This is another example of the lie social media has sold us and how it has rewired us and our behavior.

COMPARISON = DEATH

Let's say I follow 730 people on my favorite social media platform, which is Instagram. Most of us follow more. This means that *every day of the year* my account would theoretically show me photos from two people who are having the best day of their year (730 people divided by 365 days = 2). We usually post more if we're having an incredible experience or a phenomenal trip, so it probably means more than two posts. It also means that *every day of the year*, sixty-one of the people I follow are having the best day of their month (730 divided by twelve months = sixty-one). Every day on my feed, sixty-one people are having the best day of their month, and two people are having the best day of their year. So when I look at Instagram every day, my feed is flooded with images of people who appear to be having their best day of their month, year, or maybe even their life. How can I *not* feel like my life isn't measuring up?

We have front row seats to peoples' best days—every day. And it looks like everyone is having a blast and living life to the fullest. I am inundated with people lounging on vacations in exotic locations around the world, or hiking with their special someone in an incredibly picturesque location, or laughing their heads off at social functions, all of them appearing to have the absolute time of their lives. Not many people post sad or lonely posts; I know I don't. People have said to me, "Pete, you lead such an exciting life!" I usually laugh nervously and mutter something about only posting the exciting stuff. The highlights. I don't post when I'm home alone on a Saturday night. Maybe I should.

It's not exactly breaking news that most people on social media tend to make things seem better than they actually are. It's a phenomenon called *image curation*. We curate images of ourselves because we control everything we post. We doctor photos with filters, angles, and poses. It's like the difference between a tagged photo and a profile pic. Tagged photos of ourselves are nearly unrecognizable; we didn't even know we were capable of looking like an alien under stress. I've never looked at a photo I was tagged in and thought, *Man, I look good in that one!* Usually, my reaction is closer to something like, *Wow was I in physical pain? Did someone punch me in the stomach right before that pic!?* But somehow in our profile pics, we look like models and celebrities.

Not only do we see people's best days, but we also compare our worst days with their best. Heads up: sports analogy forthcoming. Game film is a recording of every play of an entire game. Many athletes use this film to review and examine opportunities for improvement. In contrast, the highlight reel is a much shorter recording that only captures an athlete's extraordinary plays in a game. On social media, we compare our game film (our everyday lives) to other people's highlight reels (the best days of other people's lives). Before the advent of the smartphone, people only knew what they saw firsthand or what their friends told them. While comparisons still existed, they were limited. But today, we compare our everyday lives with the highlights of everyone else's, and we can do it twenty-four hours a day. The content and inevitable comparisons never end.

At the end of the day, we should only compare ourselves to ourselves. This self-comparison is not a thief of joy but a key to growth. Compare yourself to who you were yesterday. Compare yourself to who you were last week, last month, last year. Not to anyone else. Are you growing? Are you challenging yourself? Are you improving as a person? Maybe you don't like who you are today compared to who you were last year. You can work toward becoming the person you want to be, and you can start today.

How does social media make you feel? Personally, it often makes me feel "less than," overwhelmed, and inferior. Like my life is lame, boring, and insignificant. I'm almost never glad after having looked at social media—except when I find that perfect, hilarious meme. I usually feel worse. And my reaction isn't singular: over half of 18 to 34-year-olds said their social media feed makes them feel jealous and ugly, and 30 percent said lonely.[77] So why do we keep scrolling and scrolling and scrolling? Why do so many of us wake up and feel a fiendish, gravitational pull to check our phones?

ENGINEERED TO ADDICT

Likes, comments, and shares have become a social currency from which we derive our significance, value, and happiness. I have conditioned myself to feel better when I get more likes on a post. I have made myself a product and given others the power to approve or reject me. I have become preoccupied with the opinions of others, even going so far as to allow their opinions to contribute to my identity. Over 93 million selfies are taken every day on Android devices alone, and one study reported that for people ages 18 to 24, every third photo they took was a selfie.[78] Believe it or not, more than two hundred fifty people have died while taking selfies.[79] We are literally selfie-ing ourselves to death.

FOMO (fear of missing out) and FOBO (fear of better options) are real and have been diagnosed as social anxieties. In a university study, seven out of ten college students said they would give up social media if not for a fear of being left out or of missing out: "For me, FOMO and FOBO are real. When I see what's online, I start comparing myself to those people … and when I'm offline, I imagine what other kids are saying."[80] Sound familiar? We now have this portal that allows us to see what all our friends are doing morning, noon, and night.

By design, social media is highly addictive. The tech execs and people who invented and developed social media and modern technological devices don't even let their own kids use them. Steve Jobs was once asked about his kids loving the iPad, to which he replied, "Actually we don't allow the iPad in the home. We think it's too dangerous for them in effect."[81] Bill Gates, Steve Jobs, Marissa Mayer, Mark Zuckerberg, and others have refused to give their own kids the mobile devices and apps that they themselves create. Or if they don't completely abstain, they strictly limit their kids' screen time. Let me repeat this for emphasis: the tech moguls and founders who invented social media have banned their own children from using it.[82] This should send us a message—loud and clear. Social media is a product that was deliberately engineered to make us crave and physically need it. The very definition of addictive. It sabotages our brains, our social interactions, and our lives. It is a Trojan horse. *The Social Dilemma* is a documentary about this very subject, and I highly recommend it as it's both challenging and convicting.

Whether we believe it or not, our habits reveal and shape what we prioritize, love, and trust.[83] We know enough about social media and screens at this point to know that their impact is largely a negative one. The time has come for us to burn the Trojan horse and reclaim our lives. I'm not suggesting that we go cold turkey and swear off social media for good, but I am strongly advocating that *we* learn to use *it* instead of allowing *it* to use *us*. We have to figure out how to get the best out of social media without it getting the best of us.

If you have an iPhone and ever attempted to organize your social media apps into a folder, you may have noticed that its programming places these apps into a folder labeled "Productivity" by default. Could anything be further from the truth? Social media apps present serious obstacles to productivity and personal accomplishments. Your phone is a tool, not a boss. "Coach Tony" wrote one of the best articles I've ever read about how to set up your phone for maximum productivity, focus, and even increased life expectancy.[84] It's a long list, but it's worth checking out. Here are some more tips to disarm the Trojan horse. We recommend starting with one or two and then building from there.

Tips for Healthy Social Media Use

1. Schedule social media time throughout the day where you consciously allow yourself to use social media. Fifteen-minute blocks work well. Set a maximum time allowed per app and limit it using Rescuetime (for laptops/desktops only), Break Free, Moment, or a similar app.

2. Utilize the airplane mode button early and often, or put your phone on silent and set it out of arm's reach. Check your Screen Time in your weekly evaluation. Set a goal to use it less.

3. Turn off all social media notifications. I have done this, and it is a game changer.

4. Engage your social media with purpose and gratitude. Be grateful for blessings in loved ones' lives. Use other posts for inspiration and motivation, not comparison.

5. Become a person of pause. Pause before posting or replying to a post. Ask yourself if it's really worth it. Are you edifying and building people up or are you tearing people down?

6. Make your bedroom a "social media free" zone. Don't look at social media for the first two hours of the day or the last hour before bed.

7. Move social media apps off your home screen and into a folder where they are more difficult to access. Then move them to the second page of that folder. Title this folder "Playtime," "Amusement," "Wasting time," or "Recess" to remind yourself of its true purpose.

8. Block off your day so that you have chunks of time for being creative and working without interruption. Then have other blocks dedicated to rapid task processing, like sending emails. Along with this, you can even use social media as a reward for getting something done.

9. Have a regular time of "fasting" from technology. Fasting is abstaining from something. This can be weekly, bi-weekly, or monthly at the very least. Personally, I think it needs to be more

often than that. Shoot a bullet before a cannonball. Start with a "selfie fast" for a week.

10. Unfollow accounts that make you feel bad about yourself. Remember that most posts are carefully curated and not reflective of real life.

For most of us, massive, ruthless, drastic action will be needed around social media because of the grip it has on our lives. I knew someone who was so serious about reclaiming her life from social media that she deleted all social media apps from her phone and either used her web browser or her laptop to look at social media. She still used it and posted from time to time, and she said her life was ten times better. Her actions are a powerful example of how to assert yourself over social media and responsibly prioritize your time and well-being.

BIG IDEA

We know social media accomplishes positive things. It can instantly connect us with people around the world, and it offers another method of expression—often helping users discover gifts and talents that would have otherwise gone unnoticed. Social media platforms can help spread ideas and give voice to people and groups who were otherwise largely voiceless. But overuse and misuse come at an enormous cost. Social media is a Trojan horse that claims to do good but can and will wreak havoc if left unchecked. The stakes are so high that our very well-being hangs in the balance. We must learn to use social media in a healthy, responsible way and control it instead of allowing it to control us.

7

INDISTRACTABLE:
TIME AND ATTENTION MANAGEMENT

PETE

I have become notoriously impatient. I think I've always been somewhat impatient, but Amazon Prime has ruined me. When I was younger, I had to wait four to six weeks for the products I ordered from TV to arrive. Four to six weeks! And that was with "expedited" shipping. More often I waited six to eight weeks. I think of the scene in the movie *A Christmas Story* where Ralphie orders the Ovaltine decoder and waits forever for it to arrive. He checked the mailbox every day. That was me with the SweeTARTS & Kids Club credentials.

I filled out the paperwork, which consisted of a little tear-off reply card that I found in the candy aisle at CVS. I mailed it in with ten wrappers of SweeTARTS (bar codes included) as instructed. Then I waited. And waited. And waited. For over three months. It finally arrived, and I was officially in the club. That meant that every time I purchased five packs of SweeTARTS, I had the grand privilege of receiving an extra pack for free. Instead of a BOGO (buy one get one) promotion, it was a BFGO (buy five get one). As a kid, I never made the connection that the more SweeTARTS I ate, the more ulcers that developed in my mouth. Don't worry, I've replaced them with Chewy Spree, a much healthier alternative.

Today, I get agitated when an order doesn't arrive the following day. Sometimes when a package doesn't arrive by the date promised by

Amazon, I summon my inner "Karen" and call headquarters to demand a refund for the shipping cost. I've often placed orders for two-hour shipping when I didn't even need the item that quickly. That still blows my mind. I want it, and I want it now. What's wrong with me? I expect everything to be instant. We are taught that delays are unacceptable when satisfying a want. If you feel it, do it. If you want it, get it. More is better. Pleasure now. Pain never. Want a book? Download it instantly. Want a song? Download that instantly too. Want a movie? Stream it two minutes ago.

There is no two-hour shipping on becoming an adult, especially on the inside. Emotional maturity takes time. Developing wisdom takes time. Growing up takes time. But it doesn't *just* take time. We all know at least one adult who is still very much a child when it comes to their emotions. It takes time *and* intentionality. It takes concentration *and* planning. It is not linear.

> *Growing old is mandatory. Growing up is optional.*
> Chili Davis, MLB coach and former outfielder

Practicing patience is difficult. And it doesn't help that technology continues to condition us to expect immediate gratification in all areas of life. Our phones send constant notifications that beckon us to look at our screens. We're so impatient nowadays that we're even struggling to build personal savings. Americans' personal savings rates—the percentage of disposable income saved—averaged 13.2 percent in 1970. In 2019, Americans saved only 7.6 percent.[85]

Part of healthy adulting is having a vision for your future and making long-term, difficult choices that will get you there. These choices involve resisting the frenzied temptations that entice us every day. Or as Dr. Shahram Heshmat, an associate professor emeritus of health economics of addiction at the University of Illinois at Springfield, says, "Resisting short-term reward in favor of a longer-term reward requires a capacity to envision the distant future. Having a vivid view of the future is a sign of social maturity for young adults."[86] This means that successful, productive people figure out what they value most and then live toward whatever that may be. This kind of intention requires delayed gratification instead of instant satisfaction because sometimes what you want right now is not actually what is most important to you.

DISCERNMENT AND DELAYED GRATIFICATION

Let's talk about delayed gratification. Delayed gratification is putting off a secondary immediate pleasure for a primary or greater pleasure or reward later. This is how we attain true satisfaction. Think of pickles. Whether you love 'em or hate 'em, pickles require delayed gratification. They're not cucumbers dipped in pickle juice; they have to soak and marinate. Any idea how long it takes a cucumber to become a pickle? For a full-sized cucumber, it takes up to two weeks. And that's twenty-four hours a day for fourteen days, which is 336 hours in total. And if you want to flavor them by fermentation, it can take a couple of months. Don't get me started on how deep the rabbit hole goes on pickling and how many websites are dedicated to cucumbers, pickles, flavoring, seasoning, brine, the ideal time and method for pickling, and other details. That research took two hours of my life that I will never get back.

Pickles aside, my point is that part of healthy adulting is having a vision for your future and making long-term, difficult choices that will get you there. These choices involve resisting the frenzied temptations that entice us every day. If we're able to choose the future over the immediate, then we become one decision closer to our ultimate goals. Or as author Zig Ziglar so wonderfully put it, "Don't give up what you want most for what you want now."

Still, you don't *always* have to delay gratification. The key is knowing when to defer and when to indulge. Spontaneous satisfaction can provide exciting, unexpected experiences, increased flexibility, and even help build relationships while sharing adventures. UCLA's Suzanne Shu and University of Pennsylvania's Marissa Sharif say that waiting for the "perfect" time to enjoy something can actually backfire because we have a future bias. It's the cousin of FOBO (fear of better options), and it's called *occasion matching*, which is compulsively waiting for an ideal future time to enjoy an indulgence.[87] The problem with occasion matching is that this ideal future time never arrives.

The kind of discernment in knowing when to delay gratification comes down, again, to knowing yourself. Generally speaking, if you tend to be impulsive, consider your future and make efforts to delay gratification. On the other hand, if you tend to delay gratification in the name of wisdom or discipline, you might need to treat yourself and enjoy whatever it is you've been putting off.

Let's discuss actionable practices to help you discern whether to delay or indulge. First, if you're going to delay something, make sure whatever you're delaying is something you actually like or want. If it's not something you want, deferring gratification can actually increase your dislike.[88] Second, make sure you delay gratification in the vitally important arenas of life, particularly health, relationships, and finances. Third, turn your goals into a game. If you save X amount, then you earn a reward. Avoid delaying your gratification for so long that you can't enjoy it. Lastly, think in terms of habits. Get in the habit of putting off mildly rewarding things now for greater pleasures or accomplishments later. Make decisions with your mission and purpose in mind. That way, once you develop a habit of choosing wisely, you also feel the freedom to splurge or cheat from time to time. You only get one shot at this life, so make it a fun one.

TIME MANAGEMENT IS DEAD

It is a fallacy to think that one just needs more time. Unless a deeper solution is found, "more time" will just fill up in the same way as the time we already have. The way to liberation and rest lies through a decision and a practice.[89]
Dallas Willard (1935–2013), philosopher

Technology and social media have been accused of stealing our time, but they don't. Every person in every country in the entire world has the exact same number of hours in a day regardless of age, income, culture, background, intelligence, profession, social status, Android/iPhone, and whatnot. We all have the same twenty-four hours, and I've never known anyone who has ever been gifted with extra time in a day or a week. You have enough time to do exactly what you are supposed to do today, this week, this month, this year, and in this life.

Because of the soaring number of distractions, putting something on our calendar does not necessarily mean that it gets done. In fact, time management is dead. It's been replaced by something new and much more important: attention management—the new heir to the throne.

The Stats on Attention and Technology

- Computer users at work change windows or check e-mail or other programs nearly thirty-seven times an hour.
- The average number of daily phone checks by people in their twenties is fifty.
- The average number of daily phone swipes, slides, and clicks is 2,617.
- Office workers take an average of sixty-four seconds after checking an e-mail to reorient themselves and get back to the task at hand.
- Cell phone use while driving leads to 1.6 million crashes every year.

These statistics are only the tip of the iceberg. The truth is that we are frighteningly distracted. Not only are we distracted, but we are also insulated. We have buffered ourselves from being alone. And if we ever happen to experience a moment alone—waiting in line, in an elevator, or even riding in a car, we whip out our phones and boom! We're no longer alone. No introspection necessary. I can't hear myself think. Actually, I don't want to.

*You can't call something a distraction unless you know
what it is distracting you from.*[90]

Nir Eyal

Scientists are well aware of our propensity for distraction and have attributed a significant portion of our inefficiency to a phenomenon called *switching costs*, in which "every time we shift our attention, the brain has to reorient itself, further taxing our mental resources."[91] We don't need more time. We need more focus. We need more attention. We need more reflection.

Attention is the scarcest resource in the world right now. You can manage your time, but if you don't manage your attention, time management is useless. Maura Nevel Thomas is an award-winning international speaker, trainer, and author on individual and corporate productivity and work-life balance, and she defines attention management as "the practice of controlling distractions, being present in the moment, finding flow, and maximizing focus, so that you can unleash your genius. It's about being intentional instead of reactive."[92]

For example, have you ever dedicated two hours to a task, perhaps a work project, a paper, or a chore? You set aside time and planned for it all week. Then the day comes, and the two hours begin. You start the task, but all of a sudden you find yourself on TikTok watching a pair of cats dance to hip hop music. Poof! Half of the time you allocated for the project is gone. Like sand through your fingers. It doesn't matter anymore if we're good time managers because we also have to become attention experts. Allocating time to a task does not guarantee that you'll accomplish it. How you manage your time will only be effective to the degree to which you learn to manage your attention as well.

In order to manage our attention, we have to operate on the defense. Why, you ask? Because a group of people exists today, and they are professional thieves. Not all of them are bad; in fact, many of them are good people. You've probably heard of them. They go by the name of marketers and advertisers. The purpose of marketing and advertising is to steal our attention for *their* purposes. Our attention is their prize, and there's more figurative noise today than ever, so marketers and advertisers are working extra hard to catch our eyes and ears—and subsequently our dollars. We have to learn to guard our attention in order to preserve our goals, fulfill our desires, and become the people we want to be. It all comes down to our attention and directing it toward what we choose.

In this swirling, churning, frenzied, clamoring, attention-seeking world, you must consciously prioritize where your focus is going. It will determine the course of your life. Don't let some marketing or advertising professional choose for you because whatever you focus your attention on will become whatever you focus your life on. Your attention or your life. It's that big of a deal.

BECOMING INDISTRACTABLE

With everything going on around us, it may feel as though all hope is lost, but that's not true. We all have the potential to become indistractable. You can become laser-focused and ruthless in this battle against distraction. You can be in control and focus on what you want, when you want it. It's less about the amount of time you put into something and more about the intensity of your focus. Some refer to intense focus as the "state of flow," "lasered in," or "in the zone." How do we reach this state of focus, and how do we stay there? Elie Venezky, author of *Hack Your Brain*, says, "Focus is a muscle, and you can build it. Too many people labor under the misconception that they're just not focused, and this becomes a self-fulfilling prophecy. Once you drop this mistaken belief, you can take a much more realistic approach to building focus."[93]

Adam Grant, an organizational psychologist at the University of Pennsylvania's Wharton Business School, says that *when* you engage in projects is very important. You want to work on your most critical and creative tasks when you are at your best. When is that? When Americans watched videos and then performed a boring data entry task, his research found support for a different mechanism: contrast effects. According to Grant's studies, "a fascinating or funny video makes the data entry task seem even more excruciating, the same way a sweet dessert makes a sour vegetable taste yuckier. So if you're trying to power through a boring task, do it after a moderately interesting one, and save your most exciting task as a reward for afterward. It's not always about time; it's about timing."[94]

Think in terms of optimization. Do you have a natural productivity curve? When do you do your best work? When are you most productive, and when are you most creative? This can vary with the time of day and even the time of week. Plan your ideal weeks, which will work out some of the time. If you don't plan them, they'll never work out. If you aim at nothing, you'll hit it every time.

The peaks and valleys of your natural workflow tell you exactly when you should schedule each part of your day, and then you can line up the tasks that matter most according to when you're best suited to doing them. During your peak hours, be even more ruthless about eliminating distractions. When your energy levels are low, answer e-mails and make simple calls. Give yourself strict time limits for both. Moderate stressful work for when you need a boost in energy and motivation.[95]

10 Steps to Indistractable

1. Control your technology. Technology is here to serve you, not the other way around. Disable as many push notifications as possible. Remove apps that you don't use regularly, and only keep apps on your home screen that help improve your productivity. Put your phone on silent and place it out of sight for chunks of time throughout the day. My phone has to be in another room in order for me to focus. I'm that weak.

2. Control your external environment. Set boundaries with others, especially in an open-office setting. Make your workplace as focus friendly as possible. Remove clutter. When you need to focus, use headphones or hang up a sign that reads "Do Not Disturb." If permitted, try moving to a different part of your office, a differ-

ent floor of your building, or a remote location. Take some short breaks of silence and solitude. Studies show that the busier you are, the more you need reflective times of silence and solitude.[96]

3. Control your internal environment. We can sometimes be our own worst enemies. Our minds were made to wander, so learning to be intentional with your thoughts can be difficult. Journal in the morning. Declutter your mind by taking regular breaks from all technology. I like to have a notepad next to me whenever I am in deep focus (with the phone in the other room) so that I can write down whatever tasks or thoughts that enter my mind. This keeps me from distracting myself from the project at hand. Do not multitask. It's a myth anyway. Focus on one thing until completion.

4. Control your expectations around communication. You need to have clear expectations around response time and how often you need to check your email. One of the biggest internal factors that chips away our ability to focus is expectations about communication. Studies have found that 84 percent of people keep their e-mail open all day long, with 70 percent of e-mails opened within six seconds of receipt.[97] Even when we're not receiving emails, it's been found that the average worker checks e-mail every six minutes.[98]

5. Control the timing of your attention and focus. Distinguish between "maker" and "manager" days. Maker days include extended periods of uninterrupted time dedicated to creativity, thinking, planning. Manager days are heavy on e-mail, communication, meetings, and other tasks and projects. Optimize your productivity curve. The data varies on what blocks of time are optimal for maximizing productivity, but a good place to start is fifty minutes of focus and then a ten-minute break.

6. Control your breaks from your computer. Take more real breaks. Time them. I have had many five and ten-minute breaks turn into an hour (or longer!) break. Make sure you resist the temptation to check social media on these breaks. This should be a physical break from your computer.[99]

7. Control your deadlines. We all operate better with accountability. Working under deadlines, even the ones that I create for myself, have been helpful for me. Find someone with whom you can be deadline partners. Tell them when you want to finish something and then give them your deadline. You will later send them whatever task you're working on or face consequences that both of you previously agreed upon. Missing your deadline needs to have immediate consequences, not "I'll take you out for a drink," but something that is actionable right then—pay a fine, donate money to a charity, post something on social media, etc. Don't forget to reward yourself after completing a difficult task.

8. Control your rest. Engage in activities that are physically, mentally, emotionally, and spiritually stimulating. Sleep more. Finding out what those activities are for you is half the battle. Explore a hobby. Find something you love to do, which has been shown to increase focus.

9. Control your identity pact. Tell others you are "indistractable." This is what author Nir Eyal calls an identity pact. They are powerful because the way we perceive ourselves affects our actual behavior.[100]

10. Control your white space and margin. Declare some tech-free zones, such as the dinner table, the car, and the bedroom. Designate times and places where phones and tablets are strictly prohibited.

WHAT WE CAN LEARN FROM A PICKPOCKET

Apollo Robbins is one of the world's best pickpockets. He performed a Vegas show that ran for years and is also in high demand for corporate events. Robbins says the secret of his act is "all about the choreography of people's attention. … Attention is like water. It flows. It's liquid. You create channels to divert it, and you hope that it flows the right way. … I use framing the way a movie director or a cinematographer would," he said. "If I lean my face close in to someone's, like this"—he demonstrated—"it's like a closeup. All their attention is on my face, and their pockets, especially the ones on their lower body, are out of the frame. Or if I want to move their attention off their jacket pocket, I can say, 'You had a wallet in your back pocket—is it still there?' Now their focus is on their back pocket, or their brain just short-circuits for a second, and I'm free to steal from their jacket."[101]

We must pay attention to what is "in frame" and what is "out of frame." We have the power to place things in our frame and keep them out. We need to consciously make this choice every day. What will you keep in your frame, and what will you take out?

I attended a conference at a large hotel several years ago, and during one of the sessions, the emcee showed security camera footage of a guy texting and walking straight into a wall! Right outside of our meeting room. The best part was when I realized it was one of my best friends. Don't walk and text! This part of the reality we all face, right? Our lack of focus has caused us to do something that we haven't wanted or meant to do. This can be physically dangerous and also mentally and emotionally hazardous. Focus is a skill to develop over time. Give yourself grace during this process of honing your focus. If you put in the time and effort, then you will accomplish the things in life that you set out to do and become the person you want to be.

It doesn't happen all at once. You become. It takes a long time.
Margery Williams, *The Velveteen Rabbit*

BIG IDEA

Time management is dead. Attention management has taken its place as the crucial skill of our time. Become an indistractable focus expert to unleash your creativity and maximize your productivity.

HEALTHY HABITS

REDUCE ANXIETY

Put
Others
First

OVERCOME
LONELINESS
EQ

Lead

fight depression

GAIN WISDOM

PRACTICE
GRATITUDE

LEAD OTHERS

Success

Find a Mentor

Assess
Your
Inner
Circle

MENTAL
HEALTH

Be Real

FOCUS

STOP SCROLLING

IMPACT

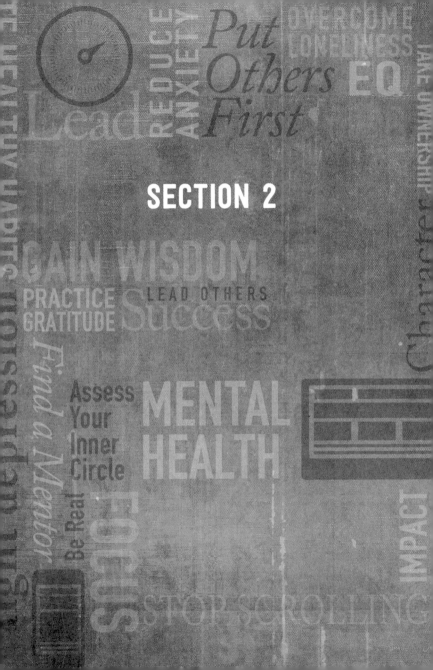

SECTION 2

INTERMISSION: WADING INTO MENTAL HEALTH

PETE

We hope *Adulting 101 Book 2: #liveyourbestlife* has been helpful so far. Before we move into the second half of the book, we want to prepare you to wade into deeper waters. Deeper feelings. Deeper experiences. We are going to talk about anxiety, depression, and loneliness in this second half—hopefully in a helpful, delicate way.

When I was working my first job straight out of college in Virginia Beach, I attended a staff meeting of about seven people. One person took the first leap in vulnerability by sharing that she was going through a rough patch and started seeing a therapist. One by one, each of us shared, and we discovered that all seven of us were in counseling and had been too embarrassed to tell anyone. This embarrassment is obviously a common feeling, but why? Why do I still feel embarrassed and ashamed that I have attended counseling during multiple seasons of my life? Why the hesitation or resistance to seek treatment? I think it can be a combination of reasons: the social stigma, the opinions of others, the family and friends who may discourage it, the legwork required to find a therapist and afford one, the pride, and the fear.

We must destigmatize getting help for our mental health. We aren't embarrassed if our car breaks down. We simply bring it to a mechanic. We aren't embarrassed if we sprain our ankle. We visit the doctor (except for the time I threw a marshmallow and tore my rotator cuff and labrum, but that's a story for another time). So why do we feel shame about visiting mental health professionals? After all, aren't they basically brain mechanics? Sure, we can employ strategies independently and see improvement. But sometimes we need professional help, and this is nothing to hide. Most of us have thought patterns, tendencies, and inner dialogues that may be skewed, harmful, or simply unkind. The truth is that we can all benefit from counseling, whether we like to admit it or not.

Even if anxiety, depression, or loneliness aren't parts of your story, a soaring number of people are experiencing them. Probably someone you know. Probably someone close to you. According to Luna Greenstein of The National Alliance on Mental Illness, it's important to learn more about these conditions because it may help us have more sympathy toward someone who experiences symptoms on a daily basis.[102] In other words, the more we know about these conditions, the more helpful we can be to friends, family, and loved ones who battle them.

If you've struggled with any of these (like we have), then you know that addressing them can sometimes feel like someone's poking at an exposed nerve. One of our goals is to destigmatize these subjects and break up the clouds of shame and embarrassment that continue to surround them. Another goal is to give some strategies to combat these challenges and help you improve your mental health. A third goal is to provide actionable steps for you to help support loved ones who may be struggling as well.

We've dedicated two chapters each to anxiety, depression, and loneliness. The first chapter is sort of a "State of the Union" to define and discuss the issue, and the second offers strategies to cope with the condition and help you discern between what professionals consider "normal" and what may be a disorder. That way, you'll know when to seek help. Note that we will use the terms counselor, therapist, and mental health professional interchangeably. Our deepest desire with this second half of the book is that it helps launch you into your quest for healthy inner adulthood, focusing on building the foundation of a flourishing, robust mental health.

Important Disclaimer: We are not experts! We have no formal training or education in the field of mental health but care deeply and are passionately invested. These topics are too important not to include in this book. We researched extensively and asked wiser, educated, seasoned professionals for their help. We recruited five of the top counselors from all over the country (with over one hundred years of combined mental health experience!) to weigh in on these topics and contribute their advice. They also shared stories of actual clients so we can hear from actual people about their struggles and experiences. Thanks again to Brad, Leonia, Susan, Jake, and Laura. Some of the testimonies included come from our friends as well. All names and details have been changed to respect privacy.

If any or all of these experiences *are* part of your story, we hope and pray this part of the book can help bring life, healing, and help to your journey. If not, maybe it will equip you to support a dear friend or family member. We've also included an appendix at the back of this book that provides additional resources, such as crisis hotlines, books, podcasts, and websites that may be helpful.

We invite you to approach this next section with a tender, compassionate spirit, an open mind, and a servant's heart. Let's come together to become a team committed to improving our own and others' mental health. Come wade into the deeper waters.

8

ANXIETY DEFINED

PETE

I t was a Friday night, and the room was rocking with about five hundred high school students screaming their heads off in the audience. I hadn't slept well the night before. My nerves had been building for weeks. The music came on, which meant the time had finally come for me to walk on stage with my friend Coby. We were in charge of entertainment at a weekend camp in New York. Both of us were in college at the time, but Coby was living in Michigan, and I was in Virginia. We had flown to each other's colleges several times in the previous months preparing our comedy routine for this very moment. We were playing game show hosts named Pep Pepperson and Buck Buckelson if I remember correctly.

Back stage, I leaned over a giant industrial trash can and dry heaved. My brain was telling my legs to walk, but they wouldn't move. My body was paralyzed. I looked at Coby and read his face—shock, disbelief, and mild panic. I couldn't go out on stage. My anxiety had proved to be too much. Coby went on stage all alone that night. I left him out to dry as he performed the routine—the one we had practiced for months—all by himself.

The next morning, we were scheduled to be funny again. Somehow, I miraculously made it out on stage, stuttering and stumbling through my lines. The only thing that was legitimately funny was how I managed to sweat all the way through my lime green and electric purple striped zoot suit in five minutes flat. That had to be a record. This had been my first true experience with crippling anxiety, but it wouldn't be my last.

For several years, whenever I spoke in front of people, my face would go numb. My cheeks and lips would have pins and needles, like when your foot falls asleep. I didn't realize it, but I had actually developed a facial tick. Whenever I would pause during a speech, I thought I was smiling, but it turns out I was actually making a weird face—a combination of disgust and surprise (quite unsettling and uncomfortable to the audience!). I never knew I had this tick until I watched a video of myself speaking. When I first saw it, I must have rewatched the footage ten times. I couldn't believe it! I was embarrassed and felt a knot in the pit of my stomach. I wasn't sure I would ever be able to speak in front of people again.

I have also struggled with insomnia for most of my adult life. More recently, I've experienced heart irregularities in which my heart skips a beat, and I'm left feeling out of breath for a couple of seconds. All of this is to say that I have had my bouts with anxiety. It's not over, but it's become manageable. I've found some relief by practicing the strategies and techniques that we will share in the next chapter. In an ironic twist, writing these chapters has given me anxiety. Still, to this day, it sometimes creeps up out of nowhere and strikes—seemingly without provocation or cause. The exchange in my head goes something like this:

Anxiety: Beware!

Me: Beware of what?

Anxiety: Watch out!

Me: Watch out for what? Can you be more specific?!

Anxiety: …

Me: [Panics and sweats profusely]

OVERWHELMED: THE NEW NORMAL

The number of undergraduates reporting "overwhelming anxiety" is soaring. The American College Health Association reported an increase from 50 percent in 2011 to 63 percent in 2018. In 1985, the Higher Education Research Institute at UCLA began asking college freshmen if they "felt overwhelmed by all I had to do," and in 1985, 18 percent said they did; then in 2010, 29 percent said they did; then in 2016, that number jumped to 41 percent.[103] Almost 25 percent of college students report receiving a diagnosis of anxiety or receiving treatment by a mental health professional for anxiety within the last twelve months.[104]

Anxiety has even surpassed depression as the most common reason college students visit their campus' student health services.[105] It's also the most common mental health diagnosis among all college students. In fact, more than half of all students visiting campus clinics cite anxiety as a health concern according to a recent nationwide study of more than 100,000 students by the Center for Collegiate Mental Health at Penn State.[106] Student health centers are overrun and backlogged. Many centers are having to resort to only treating students in immediate crisis and referring or delaying other non-emergency mental health needs.

Anxiety is not just a challenge for young people. According to the National Institute of Mental Health, anxiety disorders are the most common mental illness in the US, affecting nearly one-third of both young people and adults.[107] Almost one in five people report they feel anxious "nearly all of the time" or "a lot of the time." According to the Anxiety and Depression Association of America, "Anxiety disorders are highly treatable, yet only 36.9 percent of those suffering receive treatment."[108] This observed lack of care is a result of many factors, one of which is that many people who suffer with anxiety don't seek treatment.[109]

The sharpest increase of reported anxiety occurs during the transition to college, and the second sharpest increase is during the transition to the real world. This makes sense because so many things suddenly change in both scenarios. So if you feel anxiety, even at an intense level, you are not alone. You're among the estimated 40 million adults in America who have some version of an anxiety disorder.[110]

Lyssa's Story

Lyssa felt nervous inside every time she had to go to class. The mere thought of having to speak made her stomach queasy. She couldn't eat anything beforehand, fearing she might throw up. She struggled to fall asleep at night, especially if she had an early morning class. She couldn't stop thinking about it, consumed with the possibility that she might be called on in class and would have to answer in front of all those people. What if she said something stupid? What if everyone laughed at her? She carefully chose who she hung out with and where she went, but she couldn't control what might happen in a class full of people who she thought would surely judge her.

Lyssa also dreaded meeting new people, so her social circle shrank. She liked the idea of dating or having a boyfriend, but she was terrified. Her relentless anxiety led to stomach issues. Lyssa couldn't order from the campus Starbucks and instead traveled to the drive-up window, too scared to speak up if her order was wrong. She even felt too nervous to ask for the stick that goes into the cup to keep the coffee from spilling.

She knew her anxiety was a problem. She wanted to be normal and meet new friends, go to new places, and try new experiences, but "new" scared her to death. She spoke softly and rarely made eye contact. She never greeted someone without being greeted first. People who didn't know her assumed she was stuck up; they didn't know she lived in a prison of her own making with walls fortified by fear. Afraid to speak up. Afraid to step out. Afraid to be noticed.

Lyssa started going to therapy and attended regularly for about a year. It was a long, arduous journey, but she discovered a new way of life, found her voice, learned how to take risks, and now lives with confidence.

ANXIETY DEFINED

Anxiety is a normal emotion. The American Psychological Association defines anxiety specifically as "an emotion characterized by feelings of tension, worried thoughts, and physical changes like increased blood pressure."[111] It is our body's natural response to stress. It is a heightened state of readiness that manifests as a feeling of fear or apprehension about what's to come. It's actually a gift. If we didn't realize something was wrong, we wouldn't be aware of danger.

That nervous feeling before a big life event is an echo of our ancestors' "fight or flight" response, which is anxiety's call to action to either stay and fight or run and flee.[112] As society has progressed and evolved, our need for this emotion has changed. Most of us no longer run into large, hungry, predatory animals or face imminent physical danger on a daily basis, so now we react to perceived emotional danger. Our anxiety now involves work, money, family, health, romance, school, and other parts of life that we navigate every day. The problem is that this response is meant to be short-term and temporary, but so many of us live with stressors that are ever present. Anxiety has become our long-term norm. With this cumulative pressure, a "freeze" option has developed along with the "fight or flight" response. This happens when someone is paralyzed with anxiety and can't seem to move. This was my experience before going out on stage at the camp.

Have you ever been doing something innocuous, like watching TV, hanging with friends, or eating breakfast, and then you think of something, and a wave of anxiety rushes over you? It might be something you forgot about, or something coming up in the future, or maybe something that doesn't even feel like a big deal. But all of a sudden, it's all you can think about. People around you may be talking, but the sound of their voices fades into the background because your thoughts become so loud, as if you're standing next to a jet engine. Or you're lying in bed, trying to fall asleep, and your stomach suddenly tightens. Your pulse quickens, and then it feels as if a heavy weight is on your chest, crushing you. Has this ever happened to you? Asking for a friend …

Sometimes, when I'm getting ready for bed, I imagine a big Demogorgon from *Stranger Things* reclining on my bed, whispering, *Come in, come in. Yesss, I've been waiting for you. Time to think and worry. Yesss, you have much to worry about.* Or maybe you don't experience a sci-fi monster, and that's because anxiety affects each person differently. For some, anxiety paralyzes them. Others avoid social interaction and search for the figurative escape hatch whenever they're around people. Or anxiety might compel them into a manic state of performance, motivating them to work harder and better. And for others, it destroys initiative and fuels doubt. There are many types of anxiety disorders, but according to the National Alliance on Mental Illness (NAMI), they share these symptoms:[113]

Emotional:

- Feelings of apprehension, dread, or worry
- Feeling tense and jumpy
- Restlessness, irritability, or being "on edge"
- Anticipating the worst and being watchful for signs of danger

Physical:

- Pounding or racing heart and shortness of breath
- Sweating, tremors, and twitches
- Headaches, fatigue, and insomnia
- Upset stomach, frequent urination, or diarrhea
- Difficulty in concentrating
- Dry mouth

Worry [anxiety] affects the circulation, the heart, the glands,
the whole nervous system.
Charles Mayo, founder of the esteemed Mayo Clinic

Some of you are reading this and didn't even know these were symptoms of anxiety. Perhaps you thought these symptoms were just part of your personality. Or maybe you thought that this was what life after college looks like. Good news: it's not!

HELPFUL VERSUS HARMFUL ANXIETY

It is important to distinguish helpful anxiety and harmful anxiety. Helpful anxiety heightens our senses. It makes us more alert and perceptive, especially as we evaluate potential threats and identify and respond to danger. This is, again, our "fight or flight" response, and anxiety can quicken our reflexes or focus our attention in an appropriate way. I like to imagine that when I feel anxiety before a big event, it's my brain's way of preparing me for optimal performance. We can embrace (and can even harness) this "right" amount of anxiety. It is completely common and totally normal.

Harmful anxiety, on the other hand, can be detrimental. When it becomes chronic, it can cause real emotional distress and become debilitating. It can feel like a lingering apprehension or a chronic sense of worry or dread without a clear reason. These inappropriate, irrational, or disproportionate feelings of perceived threats can be disruptive and intrusive when they begin to interfere with normal, everyday life.

A Counselor's Explanation

Below is an overview from renowned clinical psychologist Dr. Brad Olson, written especially for you, our *Adulting 101* readers. Enjoy.

> Anxiety becomes a problem when our bodies tell us to be afraid when we don't need to be afraid. It's an automatic response. This happens with panic attacks. We physically experience symptoms of anxiety, so we start believing we

should be on alert. Our heart beats faster, our breathing becomes shallow—we may even stop breathing for moments—our knees feel shaky and weak, our palms become sweaty, and we feel restless and agitated. These physical sensations tell us we are anxious and prepare us for danger, even when there isn't any.

Then, we start getting anxious about things we tell ourselves, like This is going to be horrible and ruin my life; no one likes me. The event isn't what makes us anxious; it's the conclusion we come to in our heads that makes us anxious— our inner dialogue. It's not the failed interview or job rejection that makes us anxious; we get anxious when we tell ourselves, I'm not good enough to work at this company; I'll never get a job, and I won't be able to support myself.

Catastrophizing the future always increases anxiety. This is why dealing with anxiety involves two parts: first, we learn to reduce and minimize the physiological responses that fool our brains into believing we should be scared. Second, we have to challenge and replace the automatic conclusions that we invent in our heads that fuel our anxiety.

It's not the event that freaks me out,
it's what I tell myself about the event that freaks me out.
A General Principle We Can Understand about Anxiety

Aaliyah's Story

I have struggled with anxiety as far back as I can remember. I have vague memories of being in school and feeling off. I often felt my chest tightening and like I wanted to physically run out of a room but couldn't pinpoint why. My struggles only worsened when I went to college. During my first semester, I was sexually assaulted by a friend whom I thought I could trust. I felt so lost after that, like a bit of a misfit, thinking no one could relate to me anymore.

After years of trying to figure it out through medication and random techniques I found on the internet, I finally came to the realization that I needed to do what was best for me, not what works in the movies. Therapy is not glamorous. It is hard work. And medication is not a cure-all or healing agent; it is something that *helps* us heal. Working out, receiving acupuncture, spending time with life-giving friends, and listening to edifying music saved me.

I still wrestle with anxiety, but it's under control. One other very important thing that has helped me through my often-debilitating anxiety is to remember that it isn't a sickness to cure or fix; it's my body trying to tell me that something is off. Sometimes this can be caused by trauma, hormones, or unknown reasons. Regardless, a lot of my relief was found in figuring out what my body was communicating to me and dealing with that instead of freaking out more and panicking about how awful I felt. This is easier said than done.

If you don't like something, change it. If you can't change it, change your attitude.
Maya Angelou, poet

CAUSES OF ANXIETY

People experience anxiety for a plethora of reasons, and sometimes there's no discernible cause. Other times it directly correlates with something we are doing. Think of it in terms of a computer. Anxiety can be a hardware problem in our brains—flawed or malfunctioning wiring—or it can be a software problem—running faulty logic programs in our thoughts.[114] It can also be a combination of both problems. If you've never experienced this, chances are that someone close to you has.

We can identify many of the complex causes and factors—world events, societal pressures, the environment in which we live, our background, safety, the news, genetics, brain chemistry, personality, life events, persistent concerns about money, love, school, family, work, relationships, presentations, friends, social media, and more. Other factors are more difficult to identify and remain unknown. For example, sometimes I wake up feeling anxious for no apparent reason. It can rear its ugly head at the most unexpected times.

It's not difficult to imagine why a record number of young people experience anxiety. Perhaps the most universal challenge they face is that of money and the lack thereof. The current financial environment forces young adults who are entering the real world to face entirely new financial pressures that their parents and grandparents didn't. The job market is more challenging without guaranteed well-paying jobs, and student debt per person is the highest it's been in history. Real estate is much more expensive when adjusted for inflation and compared to previous generations, so buying a house is out of the question for most—especially since it's difficult to acquire a mortgage loan when earning little to no money. Adulting is hard.

As young adults move into the next stage of life, they also experience a tremendous amount of pressure to succeed. Schedules are packed with no margin—from academics to athletics to activities to social lives. The culture of achievement is truly at an all-time high. College students are under stress to succeed academically, particularly those who depend on merit-based scholarships or grants to continue their education. In a national survey of college freshmen, 60 percent feel emotionally unprepared for college life.[115] So difficult relationships seem impossible to navigate. Or those who are recently out of high school or college may have to secure their own apartment, find a roommate, and learn how to pay an electric bill. Adulting is hard.

And then, when they finally manage to find an apartment and scrounge up enough pocket change to pay the deposit, they have the joy of comparing their affordable "garden level" (a.k.a. basement) apartment with the trendy, downtown loft that their friend (the one for whom everything seems to magically work out) landed. This is comparison stress. Social media has bred incredible FOMO at a level our society has never experienced before. Research even shows a strong association between time spent on electronic communication and reduced well-being among adolescents.[116] Adulting is hard.

Electronics offer an unhealthy escape and have replaced opportunities for us to develop mental strength. We didn't acquire the emotional intelligence, resilience, or coping skills necessary to handle everyday challenges. So when life goes sideways, we quickly become anxious. With the dawn of the electronic age, we are more isolated, especially in times of transition. Isolation can lead to loneliness, which can then lead to anxiety. Not to mention the blue light from our round-the-clock technology disrupts our sleep patterns, which also affects our mental health. Adulting is hard.

Martin's Story

My older brother was my hero growing up. He was five years older than me and was an all-American basketball player, playing professionally in Germany and Australia. He met and married the woman of his dreams and seemed to have the perfect life. He and his wife had moved into a new house and needed more space for their one-year-old son. It was the summer of 2016, and I was twenty-four. I was in Kentucky when I got the text that my brother's wife had been unfaithful, and a DNA test confirmed that my brother was not the biological father of their one-year-old son. In the blink of an eye, he lost his family.

Shortly after, my anxiety started. Anxiety sucks. I remember never being able to take a full breath of air. At all. Ever. For six months I was unable to fully inhale or exhale. At its worst, you feel like a stranger inside your own mind. Your words don't make sense. In social situations, you're worried about looking dumb, so you focus on saying the right thing, and then you're focusing so hard you can't find any words at all. It adversely affects all aspects of life. You're tense while you drive, worried about the future, overanalyzing every situation, and thinking irrationally. You can't turn anxiety on or off like a switch. You can't pinpoint exactly where it's coming from. And I remember thinking, *If I go on meds, then I'm weak.*

I went on vacation for spring break, and it was the worst experience of my life. I had debilitating anxiety the entire trip. Most days, I would lie in the pool, hold my breath under water, and listen to my heartbeat. It was the only thing that could calm my mind. I thought, *I'm a grown man, and I'm holding my breath under water because it's the only place I can find peace.* Eventually, I ended up taking anxiety medication, and my anxiety improved, but it took a long time. I wish I had known sooner that millions of people struggle with anxiety and that medication, therapy, and mindfulness exercises can help. I finally stopped taking the medication when I didn't need it anymore. I still get anxious from time to time, but it's not debilitating like it was before. It feels so good to be able to take a nice, deep breath.

WHEN TO SEEK HELP

One of the strengths of people who are Enneagram 6 is running potential outcomes and imagining worst case scenarios. To refresh your memory, we discussed the Enneagram personality assessment in chapter 1, and it's not just Enneagram 6s who have trouble with anxiety as they look to the future. I am an Enneagram 3 and still worry (or obsess) about potential outcomes that will almost certainly never happen.

Anxiety: What if this happens?

Me: It won't.

Anxiety: But what if it does?

Me: Good point. I will overthink and obsess over it and let it control me for the foreseeable future.

What's the difference between having anxiety and having an anxiety disorder? A helpful tool in discerning whether to seek professional help is the acronym SDI. This stands for Severity, Duration, and Intensity:

Severity: Is your day-to-day functioning affected? When feelings of anxiety (or sadness, loneliness, worry) become the norm, it's time to get help. Try to do so before your everyday life becomes impaired.

Duration: Identify the frequency and length of the feelings of anxiety. When it lingers or if it happens without cause, it's time to get help.

Intensity: How intense is the feeling? When you develop physical symptoms, such as sustained increased blood pressure, nausea, diarrhea, excessive sweating, headaches, dizziness, shaking or trembling, insomnia, or upset stomach, it's time to get help.

"Normal anxiety" relates to a specific situation or problem. When the anxiety stems from an unrealistic situation or out of proportion to the original trigger or stressor, or it comes up out of nowhere or for no reason, it might be time to get help. Dori Hutchinson, director of services at Boston University's Center for Psychiatric Rehabilitation says "When your mood state interferes with your ability to function at school [or at work] … and you don't want to hang out with your friends or teammates, and you're having difficulty concentrating because you're feeling so distressed—that's when we want to reach out and help you."[117]

When your emotions or behaviors undergo a noticeable change from your normal, day-to-day life, and your anxiety morphs and causes significant distress, this is a sign to take action and get help. Other warning signs include prolonged feelings of worry, sadness, or despair, repeated short or long moments of panic (panic attacks), constantly feeling tense or on edge, isolation or withdrawal from typical daily activities, thoughts of self-harm or suicide, fears that you know are irrational, thinking danger or catastrophe are around every corner, giving away possessions, changes in personal hygiene, and excessive use of alcohol or other drugs.[118]

Another way to gauge whether your anxiety is disruptive or not by asking yourself if it's affecting the "Four Ls": live, laugh, love, and learn. Remember Lyssa? She was experiencing major disruptions to her everyday life. Consider how it impacts your daily life (live), your ability to experience joy and happiness (laugh), your relationships (love), and the way that you think and process information and experiences (learn).

If you are experiencing any of the physical or emotional symptoms named throughout this chapter, the first step is to get a medical checkup. Your physician will rule out the possibilities that your anxiety is a result of a medical condition, drugs, or supplements you may be taking. From there, your physician may recommend therapy.

Keep in mind that a psychiatrist or a therapist is not going to solve your financial stressor or help you find a job. You're going to experience stressful situations throughout life regardless; that's true for all of us. However, as Lisa Smith, the Director of Boston University's Center for Anxiety explains, it's often "more important to manage your emotional reaction to stress than to try to change the stressful situation, which may not be fully under your control."[119] If you're at risk or endangered in some way, it is, of course, more important to remove yourself from that situation as soon as possible.

BIG IDEA

The number of people experiencing anxiety is dramatically and steadily increasing. If you are experiencing severe anxiety, rest assured that you are anything but alone. There is hope! In the next chapter, we offer specific, practical tools to help you cope with and perhaps even overcome anxiety.

9

ANXIETY OVERCOME

PETE

Anxiety: This is too much.

Me: What is?

Anxiety: All of this.

Me: But I'm not doing anything.

Anxiety: It's too much!

I f you've ever felt this way (like I have … often), we have good news. Actually, it's great news! Anxiety is highly treatable. Almost all people who put the strategies listed in this chapter into practice or seek professional help report a decrease in their anxiety and improvement in their mental health.

Hopefully, this chapter will equip you with practical tools to help you or someone you know make progress in reducing and coping with anxiety. No two people are exactly alike, and countless factors influence how effective any particular action may be. Please experiment with these strategies and find the recipe that works for you. But remember that nearly everyone who seeks help finds it.

NO CURE-ALL

When people ask me, "Pete, how do you deal with or manage your anxiety?" I usually respond, "Poorly." I've stumbled and bumbled for a while but have found techniques that help. For me, there hasn't been that one thing—that cure-all—that solved everything. Counseling was instrumental as well as surrounding myself with supportive friends who remind me what is true in reality. It's a work in progress. *I'm* a work in progress.

I once heard someone say that she always listed California, or CA, as her state of residency on surveys, which confused me because she lived in Virginia. When I asked her why she did that, she said it stood for "Constant Anxiety." That made me laugh, albeit nervously, because it was true for me too. One of the most helpful things I learned was to distinguish between what I can control and what I cannot. Most things I can't control, but I can control my response to them, how I cope with them, and how often I think about them. See, I have a tendency to obsess over certain things, like being turned down for a job or a date, or when I feel I've been "wronged." An esteemed counselor friend of mine once offered me a solution for not only my specific anxieties but also general anxiety, and it's a solution many of us don't like: we simply have to push through and build up our capacity to tolerate situations we find unpleasant. I certainly have done this in my journey, and it hasn't been pleasant. But little by little, over time, a little becomes a lot.

Imagine a bucket sitting on a frozen lake. The strategies we are about to share are like putting drops of water into that bucket. The first time you put a drop in the bucket, nothing happens. Same for the second and third drop. You keep filling the bucket, drop by drop, and eventually the bucket contains enough weight to break through the ice—not that you want to fall into icy waters. Too many people stop short of a breakthrough.

We asked five experts for their best advice on how to cope with anxiety and combined their responses with a hefty amount of research. Here are the top seven strategies we found.

7 STRATEGIES FOR BATTLING ANXIETY

Reduce Screen Use

Take an inventory of all your technology, screen, and social media use. Now take a break from it! People (myself included) often take short breaks from work by scrolling through Instagram, Snapchat, TikTok, Twitter, or Facebook, and this habit appears to be doing more harm than good. Studies have found that the more someone uses social media, the more anxious they become, and the more likely they are to have an anxiety disorder.[120] Please remember that most of what you see on television and on social media is a false reality. Most people appear flawless and carefree when this is plainly not true. What we see are curated, literally filtered images of real things. We mentioned this in an earlier chapter, but if you have an iPhone, the already-installed feature called Screen Time can be helpful. Make a goal to reduce your use by a small, manageable amount this week.

I am personally convinced that a huge contributing factor to our society's collective anxiety is our excessive technology use. I have tried 48-hour technology fasts several times and highly recommend them. I admittedly broke down and cheated after exhibiting classic symptoms of withdrawal, but after the first twenty-four hours, it was amazing. My thoughts were clearer, I felt more at peace, and I was able to listen better and be truly present. I still panicked when I would reflexively reach for my phone and not feel it in my pocket, but then I would remember it was on airplane mode, in my room, and perfectly safe. I would breathe a sigh of relief, keep calm, and carry on.

Practice Self-Care

Many people struggle to maintain healthy eating habits, consistent exercise, and regular sleep schedules during times of transition or change in their lives—new job, new home, new city, new significant other, new kids. Prioritizing your self-care behaviors becomes extremely important for maintaining your life's natural rhythms and helping you cope with stress. Some people feel a sense of guilt for taking care of themselves, but it is critical to learn and implement these self-care practices and to develop healthy habits around them.

Sleep. Set a consistent bedtime and wake-up time each day. Avoid using your bed for any activities that don't belong in bed. Avoid caffeine in the evening and monitor your alcohol intake, as both interfere with restful sleep. Take a hot shower or bath in the evening and allow yourself to relax.

Rest. Create some margin in your life. Avoid overfilling your calendar. Try not to stack appointments without allowing for some breathing room.

Exercise. If you're able, exercise is a huge help. Thirty minutes of exercise per day at whatever level of fitness you are will make a world of difference. It's been shown to have similar effects as antidepressants, as it helps the brain produce natural mood-stabilizing chemicals and develop healthy coping mechanisms.

Diet. Eat well. That means real fruits and vegetables. Reduce your sugar intake, specifically processed sugars. Pay attention to what you're eating, especially the first meal of the day, as it can set the course and tone for the rest of your day. Avoid eating late at night. Think of your body as a finely tuned sports car. You want to fuel it with premium gasoline in order to run at optimal speed.

Detox. Reduce or remove any chemicals from your body that increase or heighten symptoms of anxiety. Again, reduce caffeine. Eliminate nicotine. Avoid stimulants such as those found in energy drinks. Be careful of any natural or homeopathic supplements that may increase symptoms of anxiety. Only take medications prescribed by your doctor and take them correctly. Talk to your doctor if you experience anxiety as a side effect of any of them.

Acknowledge Your Anxiety

Identify it. Recognize it. Let anxiety know you see it and feel it and acknowledge its presence. Let's revisit the car analogy. Anxiety is allowed to be in the car; it can even be loud and obnoxious, but it isn't allowed to drive the car. You are the driver. Don't just listen to your thoughts but speak to them. You don't have to control your thoughts and feelings; you just have to keep them from controlling you. Feelings are great friends but terrible bosses. I've had times, especially during college and in my twenties, when I remember being so anxious that I couldn't eat, sleep, or function. It was paralyzing. Then I remember times when my anxiety had the opposite effect and actually propelled me into a manic state of action—trying to get more done, do things better, and work harder. Give yourself permission to feel the weight of your reality. Keeping your feelings and struggles bottled up inside is like trying to keep a beach ball underwater. It's going to surface no matter how hard you try to hold it down. What's in the well comes up in the bucket.

Remember my embarrassing story of stage fright from the last chapter? I honestly thought I might never get on a stage again. Oddly enough, I've been speaking in front of groups for a long time now. After I started acknowledging anxiety's presence, it got a little better. The intensity started to subside. It was still very much there, but it wasn't driving the car; I was. I still have some anxiety, but I allow those nervous feelings to increase my alertness and help my performance instead of inhibit it. It took a lot of practice, but it's become helpful anxiety, not harmful. Public speaking is now something that I genuinely look forward to doing. Be afraid and step into it anyway. Nobody gets over a fear of heights by standing on the ground.

Don't Fear the Label

It's okay to not be okay. Anxiety is common for people in late adolescence. The name simply describes what we're experiencing. It's not a disease to be feared or a label to define us. For many, it's not a permanent diagnosis. Taking medication for it is not necessarily a life sentence. Attack it. Be ruthless about trying new coping strategies.

No need to hurry. No need to sparkle. No need to be anybody but oneself.
Virginia Woolf (1882–1941), author

Practice Deep Breathing

You might be tempted to skip this one. I know I was. It sounds silly, but focused breathing is the number one preventative measure for anxiety. We take up to twenty-three thousand breaths every day, and if we work on this, we can move the needle. Anxiety literally takes our breath away, so take it back.

One technique is called square breathing, also known as box breathing. Slowly inhale deep breaths while counting to five. Then hold it while counting to five. Slowly let it out while counting to five. Once it's out, count to five. Repeat ten times. Or, try belly breathing: "If you ever watch children sleep, they all breathe from the belly and not the chest. This relaxed state is the more normal way to breathe," says Dr. Katherine Rosa of the Harvard-affiliated Benson-Henry Institute for Mind and Body Medicine. If you've never tried this before, try this exercise: sit in a chair, lean forward, and place your elbows on your knees. Then breathe naturally. Or put one hand on your chest, the other one on your belly, and then take deep breaths. You want the chest hand to remain still and the belly hand to move out.[121] YouTube also has tons of videos from professionals showing you how to practice controlled breathing.

You can also try prayer and/or meditation, which research shows reduce anxiety as well. Calm your thoughts. Calm your senses. Calm your brain. Simply focus on being in the here and now, not the unpredictable future. The more we appreciate this moment, the less we worry about the next.

Connect with Others

Ask for help. Find a trusted friend or confidant. Isolation can be a trigger for anxiety, so get connected with a community. Positive relationships are often a key element in this healing and maturation process. Most people, when given the chance to express how they feel and what they're struggling with, find relief and hope. Do you have honest people in your immediate circle of relationships with whom you're comfortable and who ask you questions about your life?

If you are a person of faith, look to your place of worship for support. You can't do this alone, and you weren't meant to. We all need people to help us process, mature, and cheer us on. Support from healthy community members is essential to any self-care plan when combating mental health issues, especially depression and anxiety. Healthy community members could be individuals who are in recovery for depression and anxiety, understand what boundaries look like, and have the ability to recognize when you are not your usual self.

Seek Professional Help

When anxiety gets big enough and isn't getting better, see a counselor or therapist. Anxiety is the second most common issue for people who seek counseling and therapy. Counselors and therapists are professionally trained to help us battle anxiety, and these forms of treatment are often the most effective option: "Anxiety therapy—unlike anxiety medication—treats more than just the symptoms of the problem. Therapy can help you uncover the underlying causes of your worries and fears. … Therapy gives you tools to overcome anxiety."[122]

If you're a person of faith, the first place to look for a counselor is your place of worship. Talk to someone you trust or a mentor and ask if they can recommend anyone. Your place of worship may even offer resources.

Many companies offer counseling services for their employees as part of their health benefits. Some offer special services for new employees as part of orientation. If you are in college or graduate school, almost every school offers free resources for their students. You can even seek counseling from the comfort of your own home now. Services like Talkspace, an online therapy company, match you with a therapist with whom you can text and even video chat.

Juliet's Story

Juliet had always been a high achiever. Earning good grades in high school and college was not a problem for her. She was smart, and she certainly worked hard enough, but that was the problem: she worked too hard. She was desperate to please her parents and prove that she was just as good as her brother, an Ivy League superstar. It was difficult to compete with him, but that never stopped her from trying. She was a classic perfectionist and the person who people looked to for help. Instead of going to parties and hanging out with friends, she usually studied. She felt trapped, as if she had no other choice.

After college, work became a new challenge. She struggled with not always being the top performer at her company. She would tell herself that was okay, that nothing bad would happen, and that she would be fine, but she couldn't fall asleep at night. She lay in bed feeling pressure in her chest, unable to relax, her body exhausted, but her mind very much awake and gripped with fear of failure. She was familiar with this feeling and had dealt with it ever since she was young. She kept pushing, trying harder, and doing more, all while living in fear of making a mistake and worrying her best might not be good enough. Anything short of perfection was failure in her eyes.

Juliet entered counseling, which proved to be a three-steps-forward, two-steps-back kind of deal. But as she started to recognize and combat that inner voice that told her she wasn't good enough, she felt a little better. Her compulsion to work herself into the ground started to subside. When it comes to anxiety, the biggest reality check is learning that even though the anxiety can feel awful, as if it might even kill you, it won't. Eventually, Juliet feared her anxiety less because she acquired tools in counseling to survive it.

Let everything happen to you
Beauty and terror
Just keep going
No feeling is final.
Rainer Marie Rilke (1875–1926), German poet

BONUS STRATEGIES

Here is a list of even more strategies for coping with and overcoming anxiety. Special shoutout to acclaimed clinical psychologist Dr. Brad Olson for the lion's share of this list.

- Ground yourself in the present. Focusing on the unknown future increases anxiety. Focus on each of the senses in this moment. What do you hear? What do you see? What do you smell? What does it feel like where you are sitting or standing? What taste is in your mouth? Say these things out loud. Practice mindfulness, defined by Dr. Tim Elmore as "the basic human ability to be fully present, aware of where we are and what we're doing."[123] If you find it difficult to focus on the present, some people have reported that wearing a sleep mask for a minute or two while they meditate can help.

If you want to conquer the anxiety of life, live in the moment, live in the breath.
Amit Ray, teacher of meditation, yoga, and other spiritual practices

- Role play with a friend(s). If a specific situation is giving you trouble, such as interviewing, giving presentations, or having tough interpersonal conversations, then role playing with a friend can lessen your stress and increase your confidence.
- Accept the worst that can happen. If I can imagine the worst possible thing that could happen (which most likely won't) and accept it, then I can worry about it less. Think of the worst-case scenario and then ask yourself, Can I live with this? What would I do next if that did happen? Reflect on the things in life that are out of your control and practice acceptance.

We suffer more often in imagination than in reality.
Seneca, ancient Roman philosopher, from "On Groundless Fear," his thirteenth letter

- Challenge the story in your head. What story, inner dialogue, or false conclusions are you telling yourself that is making your anxiety worse? Name them and challenge these negative thoughts. The story we tell ourselves is vitally important. It is not the situation that makes us anxious but the story we tell ourselves that freaks us out.

- Differentiate between thoughts and emotions. Emotions are excellent indicators but terrible dictators. Just because you feel or think something doesn't make it true.

- Pay attention to your triggers. What is causing your anxiety? Is it work, school, family, or something else? Pay attention to what happens when you begin to feel anxious. How do you feel? Where do you feel it? Journal this information and see if there's a pattern. As soon as you notice your first sign of anxiety, practice deep breathing.

I've had a lot of worries in my life, most of which never happened.
Mark Twain

- Move your body. Exercise. Go for a walk. Go for a bike ride. Go for a run. Lift weights. This is one of the best behavioral interventions for anxiety.

- Refocus your brain. Get your mind thinking about something else. Play a meaningless game. Read something fun or interesting. Plan your next vacation. Plan short-term activities that are enjoyable. Redirect the focus of your thoughts to something anxiety-reducing.

Smile, breathe, and go slowly.
Thich Nhat Hanh, Buddhist monk

- Focus on a mantra. Repeat a positive, helpful statement to remind you to focus on anxiety-reducing thoughts. Examples of these types of statements include, "Live this moment, not the next"; "slow down and breathe"; "God is in control"; "I can do hard things."

No amount of anxiety can change the future.
No amount of regret can change the past.
Karen Salmansohn, author of humorous self-help books

- Relax your muscles. Start by slowly tensing and then relaxing each muscle group. Begin tensing and relaxing the muscles in your toes then progressively work your way up to your neck and head. Tense your muscles for about ten seconds and then relax for thirty seconds and repeat. If it's in your budget, schedule a massage.
- Visualize. Join the theater of your mind. Find a quiet, comfortable spot, close your eyes, sit or lie down, and create mental images that take you on a visual journey to a peaceful, calming place or memory. Remember to breathe deeply.
- Listen to calming music. Music has been called the language of the soul. It touches something deep within us. It can take us to another place, moving us beyond our anxiety and worry.

Nothing is permanent in this wicked world—not even our troubles.
Charlie Chaplin (1889–1977), silent film star

- Do something selfless. Help someone with something. Get involved in a cause that you care about. Begin small and see where it takes you.
- Approach, don't avoid. Many people attempt to cope by avoiding stressors—skipping work and staying in bed all day. However, we know that avoidance tends to make anxiety worse over time. Instead, practice taking small steps to approach anxiety-provoking situations.[124]

- Give yourself grace. Do your best. Give it your best shot but don't aim for perfection.

Relief will not come instantly, but you can find stability and peace of mind. A university study conducted on peace of mind sought to identify the greatest factors that contributed to people's stability. The top five factors they discovered include:

1. Refusing to live in the past.
2. The absence of suspicion, resentment, and regret.
3. Not wasting time and energy fighting conditions you cannot change.
4. Refusing to indulge in self-pity.
5. Forcing yourself to get involved with a major goal in your current world.[125]

This is not a one-size-fits-all type of deal. That's why we shared so many strategies and tips! I know if you could will yourself to stop being anxious, you would. I certainly would. I think it's hilarious when people say, "Just relax," "Chill out," or "Calm down." Thanks so much. That's so helpful. Why didn't I think of that? Never in the history of "calm down" has anyone calmed down after being told to calm down. But do *something*. Anything. As American painter Walter Anderson wisely said, "Nothing diminishes anxiety faster than action." Be proactive. Courage is not the absence of fear, but action in the face of fear. In the end, everything will be alright. If it's not alright now, that just means it's not the end.

HOW TO SUPPORT A LOVED ONE

The increased pervasiveness of anxiety is both positive and negative for people who live in its shadow every day. On the one hand, more people are experiencing it and can relate to it, bringing a greater sense of acceptance and understanding. But on the other hand, as anxiety becomes a "normalized" experience, "it can often be downplayed as a feeling everyone experiences rather than a serious health condition."[126]

Once we learn to recognize the symptoms, we can help the people around us—family, friends, work colleagues, roommates, and others. It's safe to say with almost certainty that you know someone who wrestles with it. If and when they choose to share that struggle in their life with you, you want to be prepared for how to respond. For example, it's easy to respond, "I totally understand. I had a panic attack when I couldn't find my phone the other day," or, "I know, I freaked out when I saw the rent prices in the city." Although these kinds of statements come from a place of love (you want to relate and help the person feel like they're not alone, right?), they can actually come across hurtful or even dismissive. Anxiety disorder is a different experience from that one time you forgot your driver's license. Instead of us telling you what *not* to do, let's focus on what *to* do.

First, it can make a world of a difference to simply validate their struggle. Let them know it's okay to feel anxious at times. Don't try to explain it away. Don't assume you feel what they feel. Anxiety is not relative. Avoid saying, "There's no reason to panic," "Calm down," or "Everyone gets stressed." You don't have to understand their experience to be supportive or to console them. A good friend listens and simply shows up. Be patient and available. You don't need to continually ask if they're okay, but reassure your friend that things will be okay. Try to say it in a confident yet understanding tone. Help them feel accepted and let them know you are with them. Remind them of the reality that they will get through this.

Second, match your support to their preference. If you don't know what it is, ask. Enact the platinum rule. Ask, "What can I do to help right now?" Or, "Would it help if I simply sat here with you?" You can invite them to join you in an activity—a walk, a fitness class, a bike ride, or a little TV time. If someone is in the midst of a panic attack, the National Alliance on Mental Illness (NAMI) says "the key is to say something soothing and calming while still acknowledging [their] pain."[127] Their website offers this sample response: "I know your feelings are so overwhelming in this moment. I know you feel afraid that the pain and the problems [surrounding this situation] are never going to stop. But they will. You will get through this, and you may even laugh about it later. A year from now, this won't matter."

The third, most important way to support someone experiencing anxiety is to express your genuine, loving concern for their struggle. Gently help them seek professional help. It sometimes takes a friend to suggest in a nonjudgmental way that a doctor or counselor may be helpful. Help them find a therapist. If you are very close to this person and will be in frequent contact with them, it may even be a good idea for you to speak with a counselor as well. Although this topic can be sensitive for a lot of people, it's important.

BIG IDEA

If you're going through hell, keep going. Whatever you do, don't give up. Give yourself grace and ask for help. We are all works in progress. Asking for help is strong, so find a good friend or therapist and practice self-care. You are not meant to do this journey alone. It takes effort and sometimes treatment, but almost everyone experiences improvement when they put in the work. Start with one or two of the strategies from this chapter and see what works for you. Do whatever it takes to get healthy. It's difficult, and it's necessary. We are in your corner, cheering you on.

10

DEPRESSION DEFINED

JOSH

Like our chapters on anxiety, we first want to define and understand depression, learn the difference between depression and sadness, and identify symptoms. Then we'll share strategies to cope with and overcome it in the next chapter. Educating ourselves about depression not only helps us better understand what we ourselves or a loved one may be feeling, but it also helps us know when to seek help and how to support others who may be struggling.

I asked my dear friend Jayden to share his own battle with depression, which he hopes will help others who face a similar battle.

Jayden's Story

I can't remember the exact date when it started or when it went away, but I remember the feeling. Or rather the lack thereof. I was a freshman in college and immersed in my studies. I was an upstanding eighteen-year-old who came from a loving family and had a bright future. On paper, I was doing well: attending a prestigious university, earning good grades, meeting new friends, and maintaining a social life.

But I was beginning to feel like an intruder in my own body. Slowly but surely, I felt myself feeling less. The best way to describe my depression was "meh." I was apathetic toward everything. My first niece was born, and I went to see her in the hospital and felt nothing. I wanted to feel joy, happiness, or even jealousy, but I was numb. I had become a mentor for the local high school, so I was supposed to have it all together and help my high school age friends navigate some of the best years of their lives. While leading seemed like a healthy outlet for me, I had no one to talk to. I had to put on the mask and tell other people that everything was going to be alright when I didn't believe that to be true.

What bothered me the most, and still does to this day, is that I remember a period of my life when I was hearing ideas in my head. They weren't audible voices, but my mind suggested the most ridiculous things. I have lost friends to suicide and have been surrounded by it my entire life. Never in a million years would I consider harming myself, but that didn't stop the voice in my mind from suggesting I take my own life and for the most innocuous reasons. I'd be writing a paper in my chair then crinkle up the paper to throw it away, and my brain would think, *I'll kill myself if I miss this shot*. I felt like I was losing my mind. I can best describe my experience with depression as darkness. Every day was a struggle, and every day felt dark. I saw no light at the end of the tunnel. The opposite of hope is despair, and I was trapped in it.

When I learned that a respected friend of mine was on medication for depression, I finally had the courage to get help. The more I talked to others about it, including my doctor, the easier it became to identify the symptoms and feelings and remind myself, *It's just a bad day, not a bad life*. My depression gradually subsided as unexpectedly as it crept in. After taking the medication for four months, I woke up one summer day and felt as though I could manage without it, so I consulted with my doctor about how to wean off of it.

I wish I had known that so many people felt the same way. I wish I had told my parents, who would have helped me get help. I wish I had known I didn't have to keep it all inside and pretend like everything was alright. I kept going and somehow came out on the other side. Bouts of it return now and then, but I've recognized that the more often you are able to overcome the struggle, the more confident you become when it creeps back.

DEPRESSION DEFINED

Depression is "a common and serious medical illness that negatively affects how you feel, the way you think and how you act."[128] It takes place when you have a depressed mood or loss of interest or pleasure in usual activities during a two-week period in addition to:

- Change in appetite or weight
- Change in sleeping patterns
- Speaking and/or moving with unusual speed or slowness
- A decrease in sexual drive
- Fatigue or loss of energy
- Feelings of worthlessness, self-reproach, or guilt
- Diminished ability to think or concentrate, slowed thinking, or indecisiveness[129]

These symptoms describe what depression looks like, but here's what it feels like according to people who have experienced it firsthand:

"When you're depressed, you don't control your thoughts, your thoughts control you."

"People think depression is sadness. People think depression is crying. People think depression is dressing in black. But people are wrong. Depression is the constant feeling of being numb. Being numb to emotions, being numb to life. You wake up in the morning just to go to bed again."

"When you suffer from depression, 'I'm tired' means a permanent state of exhaustion that sleep doesn't fix. Sleep just isn't sleep any-more—it's escape."[130]

Depression can make you feel like there is no end in sight and no purpose or meaning to life. Human beings who have hope are pretty resilient, but when we lose that sense of hope, it can be crippling. It can also be easy to confuse sadness with depression. Below is a quick breakdown of some of the differences between sadness and depression. At its core, sadness is a product of a specific event, whereas depression is persistent sadness about everything.

SADNESS	DEPRESSION
Common emotion experienced by all people	Unable to resume normal function
Emotion can be traced to a specific trigger	Feelings of hopelessness, lacking motivation, loss of interest in activities that were once enjoyable
Relief is found in crying, venting, or talking out frustrations	Unable to find relief or joy
Passes with time	Symptoms last more than two weeks
Sad about something	Sad about everything
Not hereditary	Can be hereditary

Depression can affect anyone at any time, even in childhood. A major trigger event, such as losing a parent or having a family history of depression, can cause childhood depression.[131] Most often, it shows up between the late teens and mid-twenties and disproportionately impacts adults aged 18 to 25 (13.1 percent). Adult women are also nearly 50 percent more likely to suffer from depressive episodes than their male counterparts (8.7 percent to 5.3 percent).[132] There are many reasons why women are more likely to have diagnosed depression, including hormonal changes associated with pregnancy, giving birth, and menopause. Biological shifts create a fertile environment for depression to potentially crop up.[133]

Simply knowing that other people struggle with depression doesn't lessen the blow. In fact, depression has an insidious way of convincing you that you're alone and that no one understands what you are going through. These beliefs quickly lead to feelings of loneliness and isolation. The reality is that depression is common. In fact, 17.3 million people ages 18 and up had a major depressive episode in 2017.[134] This accounts for 7.1 percent of all American adults. You are not alone.

Depression doesn't discriminate. Even celebrities deal with it. Take Michael Phelps, the record-setting swimmer and world's most decorated

Olympian. Despite the fame, recognition, and success, he battled severe depression. His first bout with it came after winning six gold medals and two bronze in the 2004 Olympic Games. Phelps self-medicated with drugs to avoid the pain. After his success in the 2012 Olympic Games, he said, "I didn't want to be in the sport anymore … I didn't want to be alive anymore." At his lowest point, Phelps stayed alone in his bedroom for several days, avoiding food, hardly sleeping, and "just not wanting to be alive." At this point, he knew that he needed help. He began to open up about his feelings and sought professional help.

Phelps now shares his experiences with depression and what he learned from that time with others, saying about the sharing experience that "those moments and those feelings and those emotions for me are light years better than winning the Olympic gold medal."[135]

TYPES OF DEPRESSION

Not all depression is the same, and it is not experienced the same. It looks a little bit different for everyone. This is incredibly important information to help you care for yourself or those who struggle with it. Below is a list of some of the more common types of depression, but it is by no means an exhaustive list:

- Major Depressive Episode. This is what we traditionally associate with depression. This is when a person experiences symptoms for more than two weeks, including loss of interest in activities, weight loss or gain, trouble with sleep, restlessness or agitation, being tired and without energy, feeling worthless or guilty, trouble concentrating and making decisions, or having thoughts of suicide.

- Persistent Depressive Disorder. This form of depression occurs when symptoms last over two years. It could either be a low-grade persistent depression or chronic major depression. Symptoms are similar to a major depressive episode and include change in appetite, sleeping too much or too little, lack of energy, low self-esteem, trouble concentrating or making decisions, and feeling hopeless.

- Bipolar Disorder. People with bipolar disorder experience low lows and high highs. It's technically a mood disorder, but a person with bipolar disorder will experience depressive periods.
- Seasonal Affective Disorder. This particular form of depression happens during the winter months and often goes away in the spring and summer.
- Postpartum Depression. This form of depression can occur in women who become depressed after childbirth.[136]

CAUSES OF DEPRESSION

There is no singular event or situation that triggers depression. As we mentioned before, depression knows no bounds. Fortunately, psychologists have identified a number of factors that can increase the likelihood of depression. Genetics and a family history of depression are significant risk factors as well as abuse and loss. Nearly 30 percent of people with substance abuse problems have major or clinical depression, and some medications list depression as a side effect. Major life events can also increase your risk, such as getting married, having a child, moving, changing careers, and getting divorced.[137]

After reading this chapter, you may wonder, *Am I depressed?* Do your best to carefully evaluate if there may be other reasons why you might identify with some of the aforementioned symptoms. For example, maybe you feel overwhelmed, irritable, and exhausted because you procrastinated writing a paper, and now you're running out of time and have to pull an all-nighter. This is not depression; it's student life. If your symptoms persist or you have concerns, consult your doctor.

BIG IDEA

There is always hope. Depression is treatable. Understanding the symptoms and causes of depression can help you better sympathize with others who may be in this battle or help you recognize the battle inside of yourself. Coping with and overcoming depression will likely be difficult and take time, but relief is possible.

DEPRESSION OVERCOME

JOSH

Maybe while reading the previous chapter you thought, *That describes me*, or *I know someone exhibiting these symptoms*. We've laid the foundation for better understanding depression, so now we need to know what to do next.

The first step to treatment and recovery is to know and accept that there's no quick fix with depression. True depression is a medical diagnosis that takes time to treat, but the good news is that treatment is highly effective and can make a noticeable impact in as short as four to six weeks.

TREATING DEPRESSION

There are three primary approaches for treating depression: medication, psychotherapy, or a combination of both. As we have been discussing, depression affects everyone differently, so no one solution works best. It takes time to find the right therapist, the right medication, and the right combination. Your body and mind are highly complex, and treatment attempts to alter your brain's chemistry and thought patterns. Be patient.

Psychotherapy

If you have mild to moderate depression, it is recommended that you engage in therapy prior to starting any kind of medicine. Psychotherapy does not necessarily produce as quick of a response as medicine, but the effects have shown to have a long-lasting, positive impact.[138] Two of the commonly used types of therapy are Cognitive Behavioral Therapy (CBT) and Interpersonal Therapy (IPT).

Cognitive Behavioral Therapy helps the patient identify negative thought patterns, correct false beliefs, and change behaviors. This method has proven to be one of the most successful ways to treat a range of problems even beyond depression, and a tremendous amount of research has shown that CBT actually produces the desired change.[139] The objective of CBT is for the patients to learn how to coach themselves. That way, when they're confronted with negative thoughts or beliefs, they're equipped to identify them and then change their behaviors accordingly and independently.

Interpersonal Therapy teaches the patient to improve their relationships by communicating their emotions in a healthier way.[140] IPT is a time-structured approach that is highly focused on the patient's current relationships and social functioning. The objective is to focus on these areas in a way that helps to reduce stress. This style of therapy targets interpersonal deficits, helps to manage unresolved grief, assists in difficult life transitions, or dealing with a specific conflict.[141]

The role of the therapist is to help you identify the events (if any) that led to the depression and then equip the patient with skills to process their emotions in a positive way. Depression can go unnoticed for a long time. It sometimes creeps into your life ever so slowly, and then one day you realize you can't get out of bed because it's taken over. So if you've experienced a traumatic event or find yourself struggling more than usual, you may want to consider proactively beginning therapy, even if you feel mostly okay.

If you don't like the first therapist you work with, don't panic. Some people don't click, and that's perfectly normal. Not every therapist works for every patient. Just like medicinal treatments, finding the right therapist is a process that may take some trial and error. Don't be afraid to interview your therapist and keep trying others until you find a good fit.

Try to remain patient and know that someone is out there with whom you can connect, and they will help you get through this difficult time.

Medication

Antidepressants are the ideal medication to help fight depression. They help to correct chemical imbalances of neurotransmitters in the brain. I won't bore you with the details of neuroscience, but be aware that many antidepressants come with side effects. They also take a while to kick in—about two to four weeks on average. It is completely normal to try out different antidepressants before landing on the one that works best for you.[142]

Whatever approach you take, be sure that you are in alignment with your doctor and educate yourself on any medication that you're prescribed. Understand the potential side effects, know how long it's expected to take to feel better, and never, ever stop taking an antidepressant without the assistance of your doctor. If you start to feel better while taking medication, it is only natural to assume you can stop taking the medicine. But this can have severe effects if done suddenly and without guidance from a physician.

This next story comes from one of our trusted therapists. It provides a helpful illustration of what the therapeutic process looks like and the positive results that can come from it.

Lisa's Story

Lisa's mom originally brought her to therapy over concerns for Lisa's disrespectful, negative attitude. Culturally, respect from children toward their parents was of particularly high value in Lisa's family. Lisa's mom was angry, and Lisa was quiet and shut down. Lisa and her mom met for family sessions off and on, but it became clear that in order to open up, Lisa needed her own time in therapy. It took a long time for her to trust me as her therapist. We spent a lot of sessions discussing video games, Lady Gaga, places in the world she wanted to see, and countless other topics. Eventually, she dipped a toe in the water and opened up a little, and once she realized I was trustworthy and that it felt good to share in a space where she wouldn't be judged, she opened up a lot.

Her father had left her family when she was a kid, and he started a new family. The worse she felt about herself, the worse her grades got, which only exacerbated things at home because she was getting in trouble for her school performance. She felt like a disappointment to her mother and not valued by her father. She believed her brother was the family favorite, and she sometimes wished she were a man so that her mother would like her more. She felt like something was wrong with her, like she couldn't succeed in life. She was tired all of the time and had little to no energy to battle her feelings.

In therapy, we tried lots of ways of confronting her thoughts and beliefs. Lisa kept a journal in which she wrote all of her negative self-talk: *you are lazy; you are a disappointment; you will never succeed; you are too dumb to go to college.* The list was long. Then I asked her what she would tell her best friend if her best friend said those same things about herself. "Oh my gosh," she replied. "I would tell her she was wrong! That she's so smart and capable. I'd tell her that her family doesn't see her for who she is." Slowly, we practiced being kind to herself as she would be toward her friends. Next to every negative self-statement, Lisa wrote a truth she struggled to believe about herself but hoped to believe someday: *you are not lazy; you have depression. You are not a disappointment; you are lovable. You can succeed with hard work. You can get through college one class at a time.* The more she worked on her feelings of lovability and self-worth, the better her grades got.

Eventually, she met a guy who knew her family, knew her history, and adored all the same things she did. They became best friends and started dating. She had tough weeks, during which she mostly stayed in bed after school, self-harmed when the emotional pain was too much, and wished she could go to sleep and not wake up. But she also had good weeks. She started to work out with her boyfriend. She started doing activities and feeling joy when she did them. She kept up with her journal. She tried to believe things about herself that she didn't believe, sometimes solely because I told her they were true. She got a job and gained a little financial independence. She learned to drive. She took an antidepressant medication for several months while she got back on top of her feelings and then slowly weaned off of it with the help of her doctor.

The weeks ticked by, and she graduated high school. Then she applied to college and was accepted. She took one or two classes per semester, and by the time she stopped coming to therapy, she had completed half of her college degree and planned to finish. She had booked a summer trip to Asia, a place she used to only dream of seeing. Her face was bright and full of hope. She had energy and excitement. And when the bad days hit, she knew she would get through them and that she had the tools to do so.

Lisa and I met in weekly therapy for five years, which isn't unusual. Recovery from depression typically isn't a straight line. It's not feeling horrible one day and then great the next. It's taking a lot of small steps over a long period of time in a direction toward life and light. It's not sexy. It sometimes feels like a lot of hard work, but most worthwhile things in life require hard work. Peace, self-love, and joy are possible even when they feel impossible.

DIY Treatment

With the help of our trusted professionals, we've compiled their advice on what you can do on your own to help cope with depression.

Challenge your negative thoughts. Challenge your negative thoughts and replace them with positive, more helpful ones. For example, if you tell yourself that no one likes you, consider what evidence you have (if any) to support that statement. If that proves unhelpful, replace the negative thought with something more positive, like *I feel uncomfortable in new social situations, but if I keep at it, I will have opportunities to build friendships.*

Practice self-compassion. Be kind to yourself, particularly during the lows. Tell yourself, *May I be kind to myself in this moment*, as opposed to beating yourself up and making yourself feel worse than you did before.

Acknowledge when you are suffering, and try to remember that many other humans suffer alongside you.

Set realistic goals. Set realistic goals and hold yourself accountable to them. Then, when you complete them, enjoy the sense of accomplishment. These don't have to be ambitious, lofty goals. Start as small as you need to, such as brushing your teeth, taking a shower, or getting the mail.

Do the opposite of what the depression wants you to do. When your depression is telling you to stay in bed, get up and go for a walk. When you want to binge watch a series on the couch, call a friend and invite them over for dinner. When you don't have an appetite or want to indulge in junk food, make a point to eat a nutritious meal. Commit to using your support network in some way every day.

Prioritize your physical health. Be as active as you can and exercise. Get a solid amount of sleep. Go to bed at a reasonable hour each night and set an alarm for the morning. Eat your fruits and veggies. Shower regularly. Brush, floss—you know the drill.

HOW TO SUPPORT A LOVED ONE

Shortly after my wife and I got married, we had the opportunity to visit Spain with my new in-laws. My experience with international travel was minimal at most, so I was thrilled for this exciting, new experience.

We landed in Madrid and proceeded to rent a car. Somehow, we were assigned the ugliest vehicle ever produced. It was a brown, full sized, twelve-passenger van. To this day, I have absolutely no idea why the four of us received a twelve-passenger van.

Confused but determined, we hopped on the highway and proceeded to drive to the town where we would spend our first night. It was a quaint, historical, small town with cobblestone streets, and we showed up with a tremendously oversized, hideous van rumbling down the tiny roads. My job was that of navigator, which wasn't easy without a smartphone. I was relying on directions I had printed out ahead of time while still in the states. Then add the challenge of trying to pronounce road names in a foreign language.

We took a turn and started bouncing along more narrow roads when we noticed the locals started to scream at us. Never a good sign. They were signaling at us to turn around. Somewhere along the journey, I had sent us the wrong way down a one-way road that narrowed dramatically.

Neither of these circumstances dissuaded my father-in-law from forging ahead. He is a man who is driven to accomplish his goals and sometimes even buck the system. Despite the facts that his new son-in-law had butchered the directions and that we were clearly heading the wrong way, he continued toward the tiny exit, which I'm pretty sure was an entrance intended for people on foot. If the van was 80" wide, the entrance had to be 80.5". We heard a scraping sound as we muscled through, having damaged both sides of the van.

As the navigator, I had no idea where to go or what to do, and I ultimately went the wrong direction. This is how it can feel when interacting with loved ones going through depression—lost and clueless. Many of us have people in our lives who we love and who also have anxiety or depression. It can be difficult to know what to say or how to interact with them. We want them to know that we care, but we don't want to constantly remind them of their struggle either.

I have a close friend who is battling depression. He is one of the smartest people I know, is highly successful, and enjoys a great career. From the outside, his life is enviable to us all. But depression cropped up and camped out. He has sought counseling and remains open and honest with his close family and friends, but it is a true battle. And if anyone is smart enough to fix a problem, it's him. Watching this unfold firsthand, I have been nervous about asking how he is doing. I'm unsure of what to say, and I fear I'm saying too much and too often. Do I ask about it? Do I wait for him to bring it up? Am I making it worse for him? But if I don't say anything, does it seem like I don't care? It's honestly overwhelming. I care deeply, but I don't know what to say or do. This section is intended to help you identify a friend who may be struggling with depression and offer advice on how to support them.

Recognizing Depression in Others

As we have outlined, there is no "one size fits all" with depression. Whether it is how the symptoms present themselves or what kind of treatment works, everyone will have a different experience. As you read through this list, allow these symptoms to boost your awareness and kick off a dialogue with a loved one.

- Seems sad or tearful
- Expresses a bleak outlook on life
- Frequently complains about aches and pains
- Hopeless about the future
- Talks about feeling guilty, empty, or worthless
- Seems less interested in spending time together
- Communicates less frequently than normal
- Gets upset easily or is unusually irritable
- Has less energy or moves slowly
- Has less interest in their appearance and begins to neglect basic hygiene
- Has trouble sleeping or sleeps more than usual
- Cares less about their usual activities or interests
- Seems forgetful
- Has trouble concentrating or deciding
- Eats more or less than usual
- Talks about death and suicide[143]

Fortunately, the best thing you can do is simple: be there. Even when it's hard, your presence makes a big difference. As you begin to walk down this path with someone you care about, remember that you can't fix them. We love quick results, and we want to do or say something to turn things around. But depression isn't a problem that has a rapid solution. It is a medical diagnosis that requires treatment and care. Engage, ask open-ended questions, and listen actively. If they're not talking about it, initiate a conversation. Here are some conversation starters:

- You seem to be having a hard time recently. What's on your mind?
- Can you help me understand how you are feeling?
- I have been feeling concerned about you lately.
- I wanted to check in with you because you have seemed pretty down lately.
- Recently, I have noticed some differences in you and wondered how you are doing.

If your friend or loved one has confided in you that they may have a problem, be sure to express your love and support. You can also encourage them to schedule a checkup with their primary care physician. It's a lot less scary than going to a therapist. Offer to go with them for extra support. Remind them that they're not alone, that you care for them, and that they're important. You can also use encouraging statements such as:

- You're not alone. I'm here for you.
- Please tell me what I can do now to help you.
- Even if I'm not able to understand exactly how you feel, I care about you and want to help.
- You're important to me. Your life is important to me.

Avoid telling them to cheer up or snap out of it, to try harder, to look on the bright side, to change their attitude, or that things could be worse.[144] You may say those things with good intentions, but they can come across as dismissive and make the person struggling with depression feel guilty or ashamed. You are there to love, support, and encourage them on their uphill path to healing. Your consistency to stay engaged is crucial, and the fact that you are willing to love and support someone during such a time speaks volumes of your character. Keep loving and serving them.

BIG IDEA

Depression is a long, hard-fought battle, but there is hope. If you are battling depression, find a support network and seek help. If you are helping someone battle depression, remember to be present, engaged, and encouraging.

12

LONELINESS DEFINED

JOSH

Your morning begins with your iPhone sounding that dreaded default alarm clock tone, which is truly the worst. But it's alright because you roll over and jump on Instagram to see your friends' posts from last night. After casually scrolling for what feels like a while, you check the time and realize you're running late. You roll out of bed and hop in the shower to get ready for work. Your nearby Alexa device chirps the most recent news updates and lets you know the weather before you leave.

You grab your cup of coffee that brewed in your Keurig and run out the door. You hop in your car and slide into autopilot mode as you drive to the office. Your Brené Brown podcast fires up, and you roll into work while snacking on a granola bar that you'd left in your car from the day before. At work, you walk to your desk and pop in your headphones. You work best when you can concentrate without interruption. You resume the podcast and then transition over to Spotify to listen to a custom playlist curated by an algorithm that somehow knows you better than you know yourself.

It is 11:30, and you start to get hungry. You hop on your DoorDash app and order Chipotle from down the road. Thirty-five minutes later, you are snacking on a delicious burrito, still glued to your laptop. The afternoon flies by as you try to wrap up your project before its deadline the next morning. It's nearing dinner time now, and you feel good about having completed your project. You head home to prepare this week's fresh meal delivered by Blue Apron. You also received the new AirPods that you ordered yesterday from Amazon.

The new AirPods trump the old ones, and you are back to listening to your Spotify playlist. You start cooking, and while you wait for the sauce to thicken, you watch TikToks. You were so wrapped up in work that you haven't had a chance to catch up on what your friends have been doing all day. After looking through TikTok, you hop back to Instagram. Look: Alex and Amanda went to Atlanta for the weekend. That looks fun.

Dinner was delicious, and now it's time to settle in and watch the next episode of *Stranger Things*. As 11 p.m. nears, you decide it's the "adult" thing to do to get some rest and go to bed. You set the same dreaded alarm to go off at 6 the next morning and do it all over again.

This may not be your exact experience, but I'm willing to bet you can relate to at least a few of them. Notice how easy it is to go through an entire day without having a meaningful conversation with another person. Technology is an incredible gift, but we can also see its potential to perpetuate loneliness. Society (and Silicon Valley) has made it effortless to stay in communication all day long without ever building true connections.

Take Austin, Texas, for example. It's considered one of the best places to live in the country. It has an incredible university, lots of tech startups, a booming economy, and a low unemployment rate. It's one of the best cities in which to start a career and to raise a family, not to mention the killer food.[145] Despite this heaven on earth vibe, 60 percent of the population of the city reports that they feel lonely.[146]

Gen Z is reportedly the loneliest generation on the planet—even more lonely than senior citizens. A Cigna survey of twenty thousand Americans supports the notion that we're facing a loneliness epidemic:

- 47% feel left out
- 46% sometimes or always feel alone
- 43% feel their relationships are not meaningful

- 43% feel isolated from others
- 27% rarely or never feel there are people who really understand them
- 20% rarely or never feel close to people
- 18% have people they can talk to[147]

Let's pause and process that information for a moment. Nearly half of the people in our nation feel alone or that their relationships are not meaningful. What a heartbreaking revelation. The average American reports that they do not have a single close person to confide in.[148] Not one. But how can this be? How is it that we are more connected, have more social media friends, are in more places, and yet we feel lonelier than ever?

LONELINESS DEFINED

Loneliness is oftentimes defined as someone who is solitary, companionless, lonesome, or isolated.[149] Sounds sad but not dangerous. However, feelings of loneliness take a physical toll on our bodies. It has the same effect on mortality as if you smoked fifteen cigarettes a day, making it even more dangerous than obesity.[150]

I want to concentrate on loneliness as a state of mind. Not physical but mental. For example, I sometimes feel most alone when I'm standing among a large group of people—"lonely in the crowd." Yet within a matter of seconds, I can pull out my phone and connect to billions of people through social media, chat rooms, dating apps, gaming, or forums. With that kind of access, how can it be that we feel more isolated than any other time in history? There are a number of schools of thought around why the current generation is so lonely. We'll talk about three of the leading explanations.

First, we have experienced unprecedented geographical shifts in our social networks. If you were to rewind the clock to seventy-five years ago, you likely met your significant other on the street that you grew up on, got married within that same community, and then stayed there for employment. Fast forward fifty years and now you are more likely to go away to a university or take a job in a different state. Your geographical range to meet people has suddenly expanded, and the likelihood of growing up and marrying your childhood sweetheart rapidly decreases. Today, you can go to school online, meet someone on Bumble in any city, and work remotely from any Starbucks. In short, we have lost physical and geographical community. We have replaced it with a massive increase in communication but minimal connection. The dissolution of the local community is one of many unintended consequences of the advances in technology, and it's one element of this collective experience of loneliness.

Second, technology has completely shifted our idea of friendship. I have over a thousand friends on Facebook, and some of them I've never met. The word *friend* is one we use far too liberally. Technology has convinced us that communicating with people is the same as making a genuine connection when nothing could be further from the truth. If we are honest with ourselves, liking a post on Instagram from someone in high school whom you never talk to anymore doesn't count as meaningful human interaction. If anything, it is actually preventing you from having real interactions. One or two core connections with people who know you, understand you, and care about you have significantly more impact on loneliness than thousands of connections.

Lastly, loneliness happens when our minds value convenience above all else. Our collective inability to delay gratification seeps into every aspect of our life, not just our food or Amazon orders. We treat relationships in a similar fashion. If I experience a minor conflict with someone, it's easier and arguably more efficient to bail on that friendship than work through it with them. Now that I have access to almost eight billion people in my pocket, I have no incentive to work things out. What we often forget is that the best things in life are both difficult and rewarding. Why are we so averse to doing the work? Pause for a moment and think about two or three moments in your life that helped you grow the most. More than likely, they were challenging experiences from which you learned, developed some grit, and moved forward. Sometimes loneliness is a product of an unwillingness to work through relationships when challenges arise.

Rory's Story

Rory came from an incredibly accomplished family. Her father had a rags-to-riches story, and her mom was constantly volunteering. Both of her siblings were wildly successful business owners who married in their mid-twenties, had kids, and lived "perfect" lives. She came from a family who, from the outside looking in, had it all together. No pressure.

Growing up in this ambitious family set Rory on the path to success. However, the pressure to fit into this mold of perfection grew over the years. She struggled with things that her family didn't. She struggled to cultivate meaningful friendships and romantic relationships. She experienced hurt in her childhood place of worship and resented all people of her faith. Rory eventually felt herself spiraling away from the groundwork laid out by her family.

When college came, she looked for approval in all of the wrong places. She sought temporary companionship through shallow friendships and toxic work environments. Her need and desire to be perfect slowly consumed her as she became the black sheep of the family. This label took hold of her and made her bitter. Any time she felt that she failed someone or something, she sought fulfillment in ways that offered temporary approval. This burden followed her throughout college and eventually into her first job in her career. She needed constant approval from her boss. Any negative word and any mistake she made only confirmed her belief that she was not good enough and of little to no worth.

Rory measured her value by how many likes she got on a post, how successful her relationships were, and whether she had her family's approval. By comparing herself to those around her and failing to live up to her own expectations, she felt like a disappointment. Her intense shame bred intense loneliness. Her loneliness began to cripple her quality of life, so she reached out to a counselor. Together, she and her counselor dug up her old skeletons, and she came to understand that she was trying to find her worth in the words and approval of others, and whenever she fell short, the shame would overwhelm her.

As Rory worked with her counselor, she learned that her self-worth could only come from understanding, accepting, and loving who she truly was. Only then did she break the cycle of needing approval, striving for perfection, falling short, and then breaking down. Her loneliness that once derived from feelings of inadequacy soon transformed into a healing process that pulled her out of isolation.

SAFETY IN SELF-AWARENESS

It is dangerously easy to slip into loneliness when we're speeding through life at a million miles per hour. If I don't have a clear vision of who I am and why I matter, I can succumb to the millions of messages that bombard me, feeling like a pinball bounced around by marketing emails, social media posts, texts from friends, and calls from family. Another driver of loneliness can be the self-fulfilling prophecy of shame, but we can combat that shame with self-awareness. Earlier in this book, we talked in-depth about self-awareness and how to give yourself an accurate representation of yourself. It is crucial to be grounded in your identity so that when the storms of life come sweeping through, you remain firmly rooted.

Let's distinguish guilt from shame. Guilt is something that we feel alone over something that we have done wrong that violates a moral principle that we uphold. Shame, on the other hand, requires other people. This is why shame, not guilt, drives us toward loneliness, and it can be so much more intense than guilt.[151] Guilt is "I *made* a mistake," but shame is "I *am* a mistake." There are four kinds of shame:

1. Unrequited love. This is shame associated with someone who loved another and that love was not reciprocated.
2. Unwanted exposure. This is frequently how we think about shame. Did we do something embarrassing and someone called us out?

3. Disappointed expectation. This is when the expected or desired outcome didn't happen.
4. Exclusion. Sometimes we're not invited to the party. Our exclusion can be from real or imagined circumstances.[152]

Regardless of its flavor, shame can be debilitating. We all feel and experience shame at one point or another, but not all of us admit to it. If this is something that everyone struggles with on some level, then what is the solution? How do we combat shame and put it in its rightful place in our lives? The first step is to talk about it. Everyone experiences shame, so let's go ahead and acknowledge that we allow it to have power over our lives. Find someone who cares about you deeply, tell them how you feel, and share the experience that led to you feeling this way. Don't bury it. Find someone with whom you can engage honestly.

Next, slow down and try to trace your shame back to bigger, deeper feelings. Were you simply embarrassed for a moment? Embarrassment will pass whereas shame lasts much longer. If a friend did the same thing, would their feelings of shame be justified? Reframing your experience this way can help you determine if you're simply being too hard on yourself. Remember, who you are and what you do are not always the same.

Sometimes, particularly in a work environment, people receive feedback for having made a mistake or for needing to improve. The worst way for someone to interpret this information is to instead hear, *I am a mistake.* This happens constantly. Constructive criticism is not a personal attack. Separate those two elements. You can do something bad, but that does not make you a bad person. Your self-worth should never derive from what you do or how you perform. If it is, then you're setting yourself up for perpetual disappointment.

Lastly, form lasting connections. When we have healthy core connections, they propel us out of shame and remind us that we are all connected to something much bigger than ourselves.[153]

COMPARISON TRAP

All of my friends are getting engaged, married, and having kids. I don't even have a girlfriend.

John got an incredible job right after graduation. The first place he applied, he got the job, and now he makes $80,000 a year!

I feel like she is always traveling to incredible places, and I've never even been out of the country.

Any of these statements sound familiar? If you use any of the major social platforms, they may initially seem like a great way to keep up with friends and family. But for many, it quickly spirals into an unhealthy form of constant comparison, which has existed since the beginning of time but is a significant contributor to loneliness. And in this age of social media with the volume of sharing that takes place, the dangers of comparison have never been more evident. The mindless scrolling only depicts polished profiles and pictures of friends and strangers. You see engagements, weddings, travel, and babies, and all you can think is *Why can't my life look like that?*

Comparison is a slippery slope that quickly leads to isolation. How can you avoid this trap? Chapter 6 contains a full list of suggestions, but perhaps the simplest action is to delete your social media accounts. While this may feel like the nuclear option, it is astounding how much of your life you get back that you didn't even know you had lost. I encourage you not only to delete the apps but to also replace them. When I deleted Facebook off of my phone, I added Yahoo Finance. I have since learned an enormous amount about business. But at the end of the day, the simplest way to avoid the comparison trap is to be firmly rooted in who you are and why you matter.

To avoid the trap of comparison, seek connection. Find people in your life who you can connect with both deeply and meaningfully. If you can't resist comparing yourself to others, look for peers who are only slightly ahead of you. Don't try to catch up to Beyoncé. Look for someone whom you can realistically emulate. And practice gratitude. When you find yourself longing for more, remember what you already have. Compare yourself only to yourself. How have you grown or changed over the last week, month, and year? Your starting place is where and who you are right now.[154]

BIG IDEA

Society confuses communication with connection. Loneliness is a terrible beast that affects people of all ages, particularly young people who are launching into adulthood. Become firmly rooted in yourself and your purpose.

13

LONELINESS OVERCOME

JOSH

Until this point in your life, most every friend you have had has been one of convenience. You may have grown up together, taken a class together, played the same sport, lived in the same dorm, joined the same sorority, worked in the same place, and so on. But as you grow older, you have to be proactive and intentional about finding and keeping friends. And it's not always easy. The process of making new friends in and of itself can feel overwhelming.

Avery's Story

After earning her postgraduate degree, Avery moved from a small town in Wisconsin where everyone knew her by name to the metropolis of Atlanta to start her first "real" job. She was leaving behind her comfortable, familiar world to pursue a too-good-to-be-true opportunity to launch her career. Avery was so excited that she never slowed down to thoughtfully consider that she wouldn't know anyone in this new city or how that might impact her. She didn't realize that her entire town would be able to theoretically fit inside her new apartment complex. Her closest friends remained behind in the Midwest, but she planned to keep in touch over FaceTime. However, she hadn't understood just how different it would be.

At least Avery loved her new job. While at work, she was able to live out her passions, which gave her life. But after clocking out to go home, the sadness and loneliness set in. What was she doing? Why was she here? Doubts flooded her. She would return to her apartment, feeling isolated, and realize, *I have no one I can count on.* She also believed she was "too much" for others to be around. This mindset kept her at a distance from other people and prevented her from making friends for a long time. Whenever she needed help, she didn't want to be a burden, so she didn't reach out to anyone. At the root of these beliefs, she felt she wasn't good enough. She doubted who she was. Could a new group of people truly like her? This deep-seated insecurity kept her frozen in fear and unable to move forward.

She started to meet with a therapist who helped her realize who she was: someone of value, worthy of love and care. It took a while for Avery to accept these truths, but as the thought gained traction with her, she started to venture outside of her lonely comfort zone. She reached out to coworkers, got involved in a faith community, and volunteered with a local group of young professionals. As Avery engaged with these different communities, she realized that people genuinely liked her. She started to accept coffee and dinner invitations and allowed herself to be vulnerable with others, even letting them see her when she wasn't at her best. She invested in these relationships and eventually met her husband.

Avery's own misperceptions of herself crippled her. It wasn't until she went to therapy and developed a positive self-image that she was ready to put herself out there and make connections of substance. And none of it would have happened if she hadn't taken the first step toward accepting and loving herself.

HEALTH BENEFITS OF FRIENDSHIP

Friendships are essential to your happiness, health, and fulfillment. Harvard embarked on a study over eighty years ago measuring two different groups of men. This study of adult development was a landmark opportunity to follow a large group and observe its participants throughout the entirety of their lives. The researchers mailed out questionnaires, spoke with physicians, and performed in-person interviews to best understand this particular group of people.

The results of the study were profound. Their financial success was determined more by the warmth of their relationships rather than their intelligence. And as these men aged, the researchers found that those who enjoyed strong, positive connections were happier and healthier. The men who maintained friendships over time had sharper minds as they progressed into their eighties. Their life satisfaction was even a better predictor of their life expectancy than their cholesterol.[155]

Perhaps you're an introvert who prefers not to engage with people or at least not as often as extroverts. Even still, there are compelling scientific benefits to building friendships. Friends help you to live longer, better lives. People with friends recover more quickly from illness, lower their risk of heart disease and depression, enjoy better sleep, and reduce their stress.[156]

Lots of people want to ride with you in the limo, but what you want is someone who will take the bus with you when the limo breaks down.
Oprah Winfrey

Your choices in friendships are some of the most influential decisions you'll make in your lifetime. As you think about adulthood, make sure that you are making wise choices around the four Fs: family, faith, finances, and friends. These four buckets can make or break you throughout the course of your life. So don't take making friends lightly. They have a massive influence on the person you will become.

THE FRIEND FORMULA

We've established that having strong friendships makes us happier humans, but what does it actually look like to find and create friendships?

We asked our team of mental health professionals for help. One therapist who is greatly respected on the subject of loneliness shared her advice on how to go about creating and cultivating strong core connections. She mentions four primary components to making friends that she calls a "friend formula":

1. Go out and get involved. It helps (but isn't required) to have close core connections with people who share similar interests and passions as you do.

2. Initiate. Take a risk and make the first move. My personal tendency is to be more introverted in situations I find uncomfortable. I wait for someone to engage me. This is how we get stuck in the "friendship out of convenience" phase.

3. Be real. Maybe don't share your deepest fears and regrets in your first conversation, but seek authenticity in your relationships. As the friendship deepens, share more, ask more, and be vulnerable. Do not create a façade around your core connections. These are the people who need to know you for who you truly are.

4. Have patience. Remember that relationships are not formed instantly. It is easy in the age of instant gratification to want the friendship to blossom overnight. It doesn't usually work that way. Relationships, like most things in life, require time and nurturing.

When Katie and I first moved to Arkansas, we didn't know a soul. We didn't even know people in the same time zone as us. We were twenty-four years old, newly married with new jobs, and friendless in what felt like a foreign land. This is an intimidating position to be in. We both left worlds and friends that we knew and loved for an opportunity with Chick-fil-A. We wanted to get involved and build friendships in our new city, but we felt overwhelmed having to start all over. To give you an idea of the amount of time we spent before making friends, we watched all ten seasons of *Friends* in a month.

Once Ross, Rachel, Phoebe, Monica, Chandler, and Joey weren't cutting it, we realized we needed real (not fictional) friends. We found a home church where we could belong and plugged ourselves into it. Then we got involved in a small group with hopes of making friends. Everyone in the group already knew each other, so we had to step up and engage quickly. Both Katie and I made it a priority to meet up with people from the group to have coffee and get to know them better.

After about four months, I wanted to plan a surprise ski trip for Katie, and I considered asking one of the new couples to join us. I remember sitting down with the other husband at Starbucks one day and said, "I know this may be a little forward since we've only known each other for a couple of months, but would you and your wife like to travel to Colorado to go skiing with us?" Thankfully, he said yes, and it was the start of a friendship that's been going strong for many years now. This family remains some of our dearest friends even after they moved away from Arkansas. The moral of the story is that Katie and I had to make the conscious decision to go out, get involved, put ourselves out there, and be patient. None of this happened overnight, and it wasn't always comfortable. It's easy to want a relationship to develop rapidly, but patience is key. It takes time for friendships to deepen and mature to become lasting.

What if making friends isn't the issue? You may think to yourself, *I have a lot of friends but still feel lonely when they're around.* Maybe a deeper issue is at play. Explore the kinds of social situations that you thrive in and those that you don't. For example, maybe large groups overwhelm you, and you find one-on-one conversations more satisfying. If talking to others makes you nervous, repeat positive affirmations about yourself. Enhance your social skills by asking the person you're talking to questions about themselves. Practice healthy vulnerability by sharing flaws and challenges once you've established a trusting relationship. If you're unsure how to invite someone for a get-together, engage in a shared activity. If you both like football, meet up to watch a game.

HOW TO SUPPORT A LOVED ONE

The most terrible poverty is loneliness, and the feeling of being unloved.
Mother Teresa

Identifying loneliness in someone else can be challenging and nuanced. How are you expected to know how someone else is feeling if they don't tell you? You care deeply about them, so how could they possibly feel lonely? Navigating personal loneliness is challenging, but it can be even more challenging to know when a loved one is experiencing significant loneliness. And if you discover later that someone important to you was lonely at one point or in another, you might kick yourself and think, *How did I not see it?* You can't be expected to know everything that's happening in a person's life, so what can you look out for to help identify if someone is feeling lonely? Loneliness is a result of common root causes, and we can learn to recognize tell-tale signs of it.

Many causes of loneliness overlap with causes of depression, such as losing a loved one, moving to a new area, losing social contact, experiencing health issues, changing schools or jobs, ending a relationship, or living alone for the first time. Oftentimes loneliness can be symptomatic of a poor mental state. It's easy for the person experiencing loneliness to become frustrated or irritable as a result. Try to be patient with them. One of the most easily recognizable symptoms of loneliness is when someone begins to significantly change their standard routine or begins to neglect their personal hygiene. Sometimes people experiencing loneliness will not eat well or be disparaging about themselves. Keep an eye out for major transitions from the norm.[157]

If someone begins to exhibit behaviors associated with loneliness, don't be afraid to say something. It can be uncomfortable to ask, but ultimately, your display of care outweighs any fear you have of saying the wrong thing in this moment. After you ask about it, sincerely listen to their response. Follow up your questions by remaining present and available in the moment and listening actively. Your presence can't last forever, but your willingness to show up tells this person that they are important and that they matter to others. Lastly, encourage and support this person. Help them understand that the way they feel in this moment is not their ultimate destination but a singular moment in time that will pass. It won't last forever.

Loneliness continues to become more and more prevalent in our world as we continue to confuse communication for true connection. It's easy to fall victim to loneliness given the advance of technology, but it doesn't have to be this way. You can lead a life of true friendship and help others move past loneliness too.

BIG IDEA

Developing and maintaining friendships is essential to becoming a healthy adult and enjoying a fulfilled life. You are not alone. Take a risk and be the first to say hello. Go out and connect with people. You were made for this.

14

TRUE PEACE

PETE

How would you answer this question: Who are you? This is a question of identity, and the truth is that our identities are complicated and layered, making it difficult to capture the essence of ourselves in a sentence or two. We tend to link our identities with our vocations, which is why one of the most common questions when meeting someone is "What do you do?" How might you react if someone answered, "I promote positivity in the world"? Or "I give and receive love." I don't know about you, but I doubt I would talk to that person for long.

Most of us, if we're honest, might derive our identity from sources that we know we shouldn't. Author Henri Nouwen says there are five false sources of identity that stem from five lies that humans believe about themselves:

1. I am what I have.
2. I am what I do.
3. I am what others say or think of me.
4. I am nothing more than my worst moment.
5. I am nothing less than my best moment.[158]

Not only are these beliefs bald-faced lies, but they are also silent assassins. They are cunning and crafty and often go undetected in our hearts and lives. When we allow people, possessions, or performances to be the ultimate sources of our identity, we cannot know ourselves or be ourselves. These substitutes fall tragically short of who we truly are. This brings us to perhaps the most important truth in this book: *our identity is received, not achieved.*

We hope that this book has been helpful to everyone—those pursuing different spiritual paths as well as those who may not be on a spiritual journey at all. But a book about the quest for healthy inner adulthood and mental health wouldn't be complete without us sharing encouragement from our Christian spiritual journeys. We can't simply share life principles and neglect to share what we believe is the secret to life.

KNOWING GOD

We talked about knowing and leading yourself and then knowing and leading others. But there is an important part of life that's even deeper. It's the bedrock of healthy inner adulthood: knowing God. You can't truly know yourself without knowing God. You can't truly know God without knowing yourself. We won't know *who* we are until we know *whose* we are. As Dr. David G. Benner, an internationally known psychologist and author, explains, "We do not find our true self by seeking it. Rather, we find our true self by seeking God. ... 'Who am I?' and 'Who is God?' are inseparable questions. ... There is no true life apart from relationship with God."[159]

To suggest that knowing yourself plays an equally important role in your spiritual journey to knowing God might set off some giant warning lights and sirens, regardless of your faith background. This suggestion might rub you the wrong way because the Christian faith has a central theme of denying yourself, losing yourself, and putting yourself last, "Yet the interdependence of knowing self and God has held a lasting and respected place in orthodox Christian history"[160] for thousands of years.

But not all knowledge is created equal. You can know *all about* God and still not *know* God. You can know all about Jesus and still not know him. You can know all about yourself and still not know yourself. In the same way, you can know about historical figures like George Washington, Anne Frank, or Martin Luther King Jr., but you don't know them. You can have informational accuracy without also having relational authenticity. What we seek is transformational knowledge. It's a relationship. It's knowing, not knowing about.

Again, we respect whatever faith perspective you may have, and we understand that each of our spiritual journeys is unique and affected by countless factors: family background, culture, geography, experiences, friends, and so forth. What is also unique is the Christian principle of sourcing your identity from God. You were created in love and for love,[161] and once you embrace it, you place your trust and your identity in him.

Rick Warren, author of *The Purpose Driven Life*, one of the bestselling books in the world (over 30 million copies sold), says that to find your identity in God means that "you abandon any image of yourself that is not from God. … You start believing what God says about you." That means you accept what God says is true about you above whatever anyone else may say—yourself included. Keep in mind that the construction of our identities on the bedrock foundation of God's love is a life-long process of inner transformation. That is the true inner quest: to know yourself, lead yourself, know others, and lead others. And it's an adventure that begins with knowing God.

What do you think God thinks of you? Many of us would answer something like, "He's a little disappointed." Or maybe we think he's even angry with us, wishing we would get our act together. Maybe you think that God doesn't want much to do with you. These beliefs echo insecurity, and those who feel insecure are most often the best at hiding it. I know that to be true because I have been that person.

Would it surprise you to hear that he loves you? He not only loves you, but he also likes you. His love for you is unconditional; it's not dependent on your behavior. It doesn't change day to day, or week to week, or month to month. There's nothing you can do to make God love you any less, and there's nothing you can do to make God love you any more. In fact, it's unrelated to your behavior. His love is limitless, relentless, and extravagant.

We want you to see yourself the way God sees you, for you discover your true self when you come to understand that you are a beloved son or daughter of God. This is your truest identity. You are custom designed, adopted, unconditionally loved, made with a purpose, free, secure, and accepted. All other ways of knowing yourself are incomplete and will leave you restless, whereas your identity in God never changes. If we root ourselves in this unchanging reality, then we are truly free and secure to become who we were meant to be.

I want to confess how seldom this firmly rooted identity in God is true for me when it comes to my day-to-day life. You see, my career journey has been a roller coaster. Within the span of four years, I applied and interviewed for three jobs within my organization. Each interview process lasted at least three months, and one lasted over six months. All three ended in rejection. Three noes in four years. After this last rejection, I was thrown for a loop. Derailed. I've always strived to be a top performer at my job, earned some of the best numbers, and thought I was considered an innovator and a pace-setter. I didn't understand why I wasn't selected for at least one of these positions.

What I hadn't realized was that achievement and performance had become idols in my life. An idol is something you worship, and we are all made to worship. But some idols can be dangerous; they creep into your life, and before you know it, you're rooting your identity in them. Your idols can even become your primary motivators. For example, my position, title, and performance had become the sources of my identity. This was both ironic and tragic because I work for a Christian nonprofit.

I know that I am radically and unconditionally loved by God, and yet I still strive to earn that love. I try to earn points with someone who isn't keeping score. Achievement had displaced God as the priority in my life. This past year, I've had the opportunity to reflect and begin the process of placing God back at the core of my core identity. It has been a painful process, and I didn't realize how fragile I had become. Not getting a couple of jobs was enough to send me into a spiral of anxiety and bitterness. It took the rejection from my organization and my bosses to begin to hear the freeing voice of Jesus again. There is a special kind of job security that comes from an identity rooted in a loving relationship with a never-failing, never-faltering, never-changing God.

God's love transforms us. We expect it to. It encompasses joy, captivating compassion, and extraordinary service. But love takes many forms. Love can even come in the form of trials or adversity. Or unexpected disappointment. Or rejection. Suffering is a powerful teacher, and some of the best results come from some of the most painful experiences, rooting out our false identities. I know God differently now because of my professional journey, and I'm grateful. It has taught me a profound truth: everything that feels bad *to* me is not necessarily bad *for* me.

My identity was based in something that was temporary, always shifting like sand on the seashore. I had to keep finding new places from which to draw my identity when the current one failed. It reminded me of a Ponzi scheme, which is a type of financial fraud. For example, it can be a fund into which initial investors deposit money, and then they are quickly paid sizable returns. However, they're not paid with actual gains from those investments; the payoffs come from the money of new investors. It's similar to a pyramid scheme and basically pays the older investors with newer investors' money, which requires a constant flow of new investors.

We commit the same fraudulent activity with our identity. We move it from one source (or account) to another. We steal from one source of identity to feed another—all of which leave us wanting. Eventually our identity comes crashing down when we fail to find a new source, or a source comes up short or is taken away. This happens because we look to temporary, manufactured things for our ultimate source of meaning, which should only come directly from God. We choose immediate over ultimate. We look to earthly things that are incapable of providing life instead of receiving life from the One who *is* life and who created life. We look horizontally to people, possessions, performance, or appearance for what we've been given vertically from God. Which axis are you operating from? Where are you searching for your identity? Horizontally or vertically?

*The foundation of our identity resides in our life-giving relationship
with the Source of Life.[162]*

David Benner, author of *The Gift of Being Yourself: the Sacred Call to Self-Discovery*

A DIVINE INVITATION

Companionship is a human need, which explains why loneliness is such a common fear: "For most people, nothing awakens feelings of deep terror like the experience of absolute disconnection from others."[163] On the other hand, nothing can vitalize the human spirit like deep connection with others. You weren't meant to be alone. You weren't meant to feel anxious or depressed. This is not the way it was meant to be. And we're thrilled to share that you never need to be alone again. Let me repeat: you never need to be alone again. Ever. God is the true cure to loneliness. One of his names is *Emmanuel*, which means "God with us," and this can be your reality if it's not already.

He understands what you've been going through and his heart breaks. He is tender and compassionate. He doesn't abandon us when we battle anxiety, depression, loneliness, or any other kind of struggle. He doesn't watch from afar. He enters into our struggles, pains, and sorrows. Whenever we feel alone, we can run to these truths and embrace this reality. We can run to him. We don't have to clean ourselves up before going to him; he wants us to go to him right in the middle of our messy life. Or as C. S. Lewis wrote, "We should bring to God what is in us, not what we think ought to be in us." He meets us where we are.

You have received a divine invitation. It is a gift of inextinguishable love, but it's up to each of us to accept it. It's an invitation to know yourself and to know God. When he is at the center of our lives and our existence, "the waters of the soul become much clearer. We glimpse a more authentic self with truer and more essential gifts to bring to the world than those wrestled out of the unconscious striving of the false self."[164] When you begin to know yourself and begin to know God, it's as if a nuclear explosion goes off inside your heart and in the world, propelling you to know, serve, and love others. This invitation comes without condemnation—only unconditional love and acceptance. To surrender and accept this love is to come home. It's to find your true identity. It's to truly know yourself.

The purpose of life is to discover your gift; the work of life is to develop it; and the meaning of life is to give your gift away.
David Viscott, psychiatrist, author of *Finding Your Strength in Difficult Times*

What's holding you back from receiving this gift? Maybe you think that your past or your present disqualifies you. No one is disqualified. This invitation is for everyone in the entire world no matter your past, present, or future. Maybe you're reluctant to accept his gift because you think that means you'll have to give up other parts of your life. Something you really don't want to give up. But God doesn't ask you to give up anything that he won't replace with something one hundred times better. He wants you to receive this gift just as you are.

Imagine for a minute that Jeff Bezos, the richest person in the world, whose net worth at the time of writing this is $145 billion, decides to give away half of his fortune. He's decided that $72.5 billion is enough to live on, and he wants to give the other $72.5 billion away to a random person This gift will instantly make this person one of the ten richest people on the planet. The only caveat for this gift? You have to give away all your earthly possessions. You are allowed five small sentimental items to retain, but everything else has to go. Would you do it? What God offers us is infinitely better than $72.5 billion. It's priceless. To refuse God's gift of divine love would be like telling Jeff Bezos, "Thanks but no thanks. I like what I have."

This gift of God's love is free, but it costs everything. That's because Jesus wants your whole you: heart, self, life, and all. To give as much as you know of yourself to as much as you know of him. That's it. It can be difficult to respond to God's love because we know the way to respond is love. Love for love. If this is something you want, find someone who is a follower of Jesus and ask him or her how to start your relationship with him. If you don't know anyone, email us, and we will gladly help you. Just take a step toward God and see what he does.

I want to finish our time with you by saying thanks. Thank you for taking some of your precious and rare time and investing it in reading this book. We hope that it's been helpful, valuable, and a blessing to you.

BIG IDEA

God pursues all of humanity with his relentless love. He is the key to adulting and becoming who you were meant to be. You are a beloved son or daughter of God. This is your true identity, and nothing can change or alter that truth.

WHAT'S NEXT

JOSH

My daughter, Lyla, loves board games. At four years old, she enjoys playing with her little brother, Brody, who is two. Lyla loves to play for as long as she can. Recently, she wanted to play the classic game Chutes and Ladders. Lyla and I set up the game and invited Brody to play with us. Brody sprinted over because he was so excited to be a part of the game. We gave him his colored board piece and began. About thirty seconds later, Brody was ready to move on from Chutes and Ladders. Being only two years old, he didn't know what he was supposed to be doing or how to win. He didn't know what the rules were or where to place his piece.

We have all been Brody at one time or another, sometimes for long stretches. We try to adult without knowing the rules or the objective or even how to play. Adulting starts as this exciting new chapter in our life, but it can quickly morph into a confusing, discouraging experience. Some of us keep playing, hoping to figure it out along the way. Some of us ask for help from a seasoned player. Regardless, it isn't much fun if we don't understand how to succeed.

Winning the game of adulting has nothing to do with what you acquire along the way. It is understanding yourself and why you are valuable. For Pete and me, that stems from our relationship with Jesus. As Pete discussed in the previous chapter, our identity and self-worth are grounded in our relationship with Christ. When your identity is found in something that is absolutely secure and unchanging, life begins to make sense. Our strong foundation helps us appreciate grace when we mess up along the adulting journey (which happens a lot), and it motivates us to keep going when the going gets tough.

The reality is that few aspects of adulthood are quick sprints. Just about everything feels more like a marathon. Sometimes you're at the front of the pack, and other times you're lagging behind, feeling like a rock is in your shoe. Every person's journey will be filled with joy, challenges, excitement, and frustration. Our encouragement to you is to realize that you are at a singular point along that journey and that any one of those emotions is not the destination.

Adulting doesn't have to be scary and mysterious; it can be empowering and enjoyable. You can use this time in your life to make an even greater impact on those around you. Pete and I hope that you walk away from this book with a clear picture of what happy, healthy adulthood looks like and a firm understanding of how you can accomplish it in your own life. We hope you to feel more confident in who you are and who you are meant to be. You have a purpose.

Lastly, remember that you are not alone on this journey. There are billions of people out there who are just like you, trying to make sense of this whole adulting thing. We have one final message for you before we finish our time together: you can do it. You are equipped and capable of battling through whatever challenges come your way. Keep pressing on! We believe in you.

APPENDIX 1

SAMPLE ROUTINES

JOSH'S MORNING ROUTINE

- Sleep. I aim to sleep seven or more hours each night.
- Sweat. Do some form of exercise, such as bike, run, or do push-ups.
- Stretch. There are a ton of worthwhile apps to guide me in stretching for five to ten minutes.
- Sip. Drink 32 ounces of water.
- Solitude. Spend ten minutes meditating (I recommend the HeadSpace app), praying, and reflecting.

PETE'S MORNING ROUTINE

Silence, Meditation, and Listening

- Pour a glass of water. Begin boiling water for tea.
- Sit in silence, concentrating on listening, breathing, and meditating.
- Write down ten things for which I'm grateful or journal thoughts from the day before.

Affirmation and Visualization

- Remind myself who I am and determine what I want to do with my day before it happens. Review goals and people to whom I need to reach out.

Solitude

- Engage in spiritual practices, such as reading the Bible and praying.

Exercise

- If I'm unable to do a full workout at the gym, I will do jumping jacks, push-ups, run in place, or a fifteen-minute YouTube home workout.

Read

Scribe

Shower and Get Ready

Begin Work Day

- Identify three of the most important tasks for the day and then pick the most important task (MIT). Attack it.

PETE'S EVENING ROUTINE

In order to have a healthy morning routine, you have to protect your evening. Here is my evening routine in order to enjoy a successful morning. For the record, I am much worse at accomplishing my evening routine than my morning routine.

- Turn off all electronics by 10:00 p.m.
- If I want to watch TV or look at my phone or computer during my last hour before bed, I wear blue light blocker glasses.
- Read for at least fifteen minutes.
- Evaluate the day. Ask myself where I saw God. Identify things for which I'm grateful for that day.
- Meditate for five minutes. Give everything and everyone over to God.
- Go to bed by 11:00 p.m.

APPENDIX 2

30 BEST QUESTIONS TO GET TO KNOW SOMEONE

The questions below are roughly and subjectively organized from easiest to most intimate.

1. If you could only eat one meal the rest of your life (or at one restaurant), what would it be and why?

2. What is your favorite movie/TV series?

3. What do you do for work? Do you like it?

4. What is your dream job?

5. Who is your dream dinner date—alive or dead?

6. What is your next travel destination?

7. If you could live anywhere in the world, where would it be?

8. What book has influenced you the most?

9. What accomplishment are you most proud of?

10. What would you do if you won 10 million dollars tomorrow?

11. Who are some of the people who have influenced you the most, or who is your hero?

12. What currently in your life makes you feel the most fulfilled?

13. What do you find interesting?

14. What would constitute a "perfect" day for you?

15. What do you value the most?

16. What are your long-term goals or dreams?

17. What's one thing you wish people understood about you?

18. Do you have an object that you wouldn't trade for anything in the world?

19. What was your family like growing up?

20. What makes you weep or pound the table?

21. What are you passionate about, or what brings you joy?

22. What do your close friends know about you that other people don't? Or if I really knew you, what would I know about you?

23. For what in your life do you feel the most grateful?

24. What is your ultimate goal in life? Is there something you've dreamed of doing for a long time? If so, why haven't you done it?

25. What do you want people to say at your funeral?

26. What are you most afraid of?

27. What is your most treasured memory? What is your worst memory?

28. If there was one thing you could change about yourself, what would it be?

29. If you could go back and change one decision in your life, what would it be? (or What past mistake do you regret most?)

30. What are 2 truths and a lie about yourself? And let me guess which is which.

APPENDIX 3

MENTAL HEALTH RESOURCES

We realize that mental health is much bigger and more complicated than what we are able to cover in a brief chapter or two. The information below is intended to provide you with helpful resources if you want to learn more or if you are in need of professional help. Please remember that you are not alone. You are loved, and people want to help you.

Emergency

Crisis Text Line (24 hours a day / 7 days a week)

- Text "HELLO" to 741741
- The crisis text line provides free, 24/7 support for a host of various topics including but not limited to depression, suicide, school, anxiety, and emotional abuse.

Non-Emergency

The National Institute of Mental Health Information Resource Center (8:30 a.m. – 5:00 p.m. EST)

- If you have a specific, non-emergency question call: (866) 615-6464

Suicide

Suicide Prevention Hotline (24 hours a day / 7 days a week)

- Call: (800) 273-8255
- This free, confidential line has people ready and waiting to assist you during this time of need. They are also able to provide numerous resources.
- Anxiety
- *The Anxiety and Phobia Workbook* by Edmund Bourne (book)

- Anxiety and Depression Association of America (website: adaa.org)
  + Click on the "Find Help" tab
- *ABIDE* (Faith-based app)
- *Calm* (app)

Depression

- Anxiety and Depression Association of America (website: adaa.org)
  + Click on the "Find Help" tab
- Depression and Bipolar Support Alliance (website: dbsalliance.org)
- Families for Depression Awareness (website: familyaware.org)

Loneliness

- *Together* by Dr. Vivek Murthy (book)
- Local volunteer opportunities (website: volunteermatch,org)
- Mental Health America (website: mhanational.org)

  + Click on the "Live Mentally Healthy" or "Find Help" tabs

Miscellaneous

- Podcasts:
  + *Unlocking Us*, Brené Brown
  + *Other People's Problems*, Hillary McBride
  + *That Sounds Fun*, Annie Downs
- Books:
  + *The Gifts of Imperfection*, *Daring Greatly*, and *Dare to Lead* by Brené Brown
  + *The Defining Decade: Why Your Twenties Matter And How to Make the Most of Them Now* by Meg Jay

- *The Dance of Anger* and *The Dance of Connection* by Harriet Lerner
- *Permission to Feel: Unlocking the Power of Emotions to Help Our Kids, Ourselves, and Our Society Thrive* by Dr. Marc Brackett
- *The Happiness Trap: How to Stop Struggling and Start Living: A Guide to ACT* by Russ Harris
- *The Highly Sensitive Person: How to Thrive When the World Overwhelms You* by Dr. Elaine Aron
- *The Enneagram in Love and Work: Understanding Your Intimate and Business Relationships* by Helen Palmer
- *Man's Search for Meaning* by Viktor Frankl
- *Radical Compassion: Learning to Love Yourself and Your World with the Practice of RAIN* by Tara Brach
- *Priming: Programming the Mind for Habit Change and Success* by Clifton Mitchell
- *Rewire: Change Your Brain to Break Bad Habits, Overcome Addictions, Conquer Self-Destructive Behavior* by Richard O'Connor

- Websites:
  - Substance Abuse and Mental Health Services Administration (findtreatment.samhsa.gov/)
  - National Alliance on Mental Illness (nami.org/home)
    - » Click on "Your Journey" tab. Choose the correct option for you.
  - Psychology Tools (psychologytools.com)
    - » Tools to help those you know who are struggling with mental illness
  - Sharon Martin (livewellwithsharonmartin.com)
    - » Codependency and perfectionism
  - Brad Hambrick (bradhambrick.com, faith based)
  - Leslie Vernick (leslievernick.com, faith based)

+ Ruler (rulerapproach.org)
+ Self-Compassion (self-compassion.org)
+ Mindfulness (umassmemorialhealthcare.org)
+ The Highly Sensitive Person (hsperson.com)

ACKNOWLEDGMENTS

FROM JOSH

Katie: This project doesn't exist without you. You are the best life partner, mother to our kids, editor, and cheerleader. *Adulting 101 Book 2* was written while expecting our third child, transitioning job opportunities, and starting life over again in a new part of the country. You are the strongest person I know, and I am beyond thankful for you.

Lyla, Brody, and Griffin: These *Adulting* books are for you. You all are my "why" for everything that I do. There is nothing sweeter than being your daddy. I love you guys with my whole heart and can't wait to see what you do in this world!

My Chick-fil-A Team: You all were the genesis (and audience) of this entire *Adulting* project. I am so thankful for the relationships that we have built over the years. It is truly a pleasure to work alongside you every day as we care for one another and our community.

Chick-fil-A Support Center and the Cathy Family: I have learned so many life skills while working in the Chick-fil-A family. Chick-fil-A was my first job as a young person and has helped me learn and grow in every area of my life. Thank you for giving me a chance and for changing my life forever.

Nina: You made this book better than anything Pete and I could have done on our own. You managed to take two very different writing styles and blend them in a way that makes this book the best that it could be. Thank you for your partnership.

BroadStreet Family: Thank you for your willingness to support and encourage us to write a second book. It has been a joy to be on your team and to be a part of your brand. *Adulting 101* doesn't exist without you.

Lauren: You have been our best cheerleader. Thank you for your willingness to be the first reader and for providing insightful feedback. You have helped shape more of this content than anyone else.

Laura: Your wisdom and experience as a licensed therapist provided an invaluable framework for Pete and me. You have been a constant source of information throughout this process.

Brian and Kim: You guys are the best parents that anyone could ask for. You both modeled healthy adulthood for my siblings and me throughout my life and made adulting something to be excited about. Thank you for many years of patience, love, and grace as we were growing up. Thank you for teaching me about finances, doing my laundry, and a whole host of topics that I didn't appreciate nearly enough at the time.

Pete: My man. This project started back when you taught all of us college seniors how to go grocery shopping and shared your life wisdom. You have always been one of the most profound influencers in my life. I have referred back to your manual of life wisdom more than all of my college textbooks combined. Your drive for excellence and passion for sharing the truth with students is contagious. I am who I am today because of your influence throughout my adult life.

FROM PETE

First, I'd like to acknowledge all of the precious twenty-somethings who have big dreams and want to change the world. You can and you will! Live boldly and keep going.

Mom and Dad: You have been examples of how to love people for as long as I can remember. "Thank you" feels inadequate and insufficient for what you've done. Thanks for believing in me from the very beginning. Your unwavering support has meant the world.

Julfree and Meathead: You continue to amaze me with your partnership, even as different as you are. Jewels, you are the best person I know. I love you. Shawny, thanks for the example of quiet servant strength that you bring to our family.

My superstar nieces, Lily and Haley: The future is waiting for you. May you live fully and fearlessly in the knowledge that you are recklessly and relentlessly loved. You two are the apples of my eye. God has incredible things in store for you.

Cane and Libby: The world is not ready for what God is going to do in and through you. I am so honored to be your godfather. Live loved.

Our editor, Nina Derek: You are the MVP for *Adulting 101 Book 2*. Editing is an understatement for what you did. It was more like translation. Thanks for helping to make sense of our chicken scratch, for believing in this project, and for helping to make it a reality and a success.

Our mental health expert team: Brad Olson, Leonia Johnson, Jake and Susan Werley, Laura Knorr, John Evans, and Jonelle Frost. Thank you not only for your expertise and training but also for your hearts for people to succeed and be healthy on the inside.

It was a joy to partner with you all, and this book could not have happened without you.

Jess DeMayo Mann: Once again your voice and insight has proved invaluable. Thank you for speaking into the book and reviewing it early (even during a crazy season of your life!).

Pilot reading team: This book would not be what it is without your help, wisdom, creative critique, and your stories.

The young men and women who shared their stories: Your vulnerability in sharing from your heart has reached our hearts and will reach many more. Whether your story was included or not, your experiences had a tremendous impact on us personally and on the direction of the book.

Carlton and the team at BroadStreet Publishing: Thank you for the tremendous amount of time, energy, patience, and wisdom you have spent on us. We are grateful for you.

My mentors and those who have taught me: I am eternally grateful for the impact and influence you've had on my life. I've heard what you said, and more than that, I've watched who you are. You have helped me become who I am. Pat, Rev. Ralph Gates, Jack, Scott, Danny, Chuck, Win, Jim, Doug, and the countless others who I have learned from, I thank God for you every day.

Josh Burnette: This series of books would not exist without you. Thank you for your wisdom, steady spirit, ability to compromise, passion, and love for people. You have taught me so much during the writing of these two books, and I am grateful for your friendship.

ABOUT THE AUTHORS

Josh Burnette is a husband, dad, businessowner, and author who currently resides in Yorktown, Virginia. Originally from Virginia Beach, Virginia, he started working for Chick-fil-A as a team member when he was barely old enough to see over the counter. He received his bachelor's degree in business management from James Madison University in 2009 (Go Dukes!). Throughout college, he served as a Young Life leader for a local high school, and his passion for mentoring young people began.

After graduating, he went to work full time for a Young Life camp in Buena Vista, Colorado. He decided to return to Chick-fil-A to combine his loves for business and working with young people. He has served as an owner/operator for over nine years and currently operates a restaurant in Yorktown, Virginia. Josh is a certified speaker with SCORRE workshops and has had the opportunity to be the keynote speaker for Verizon Wireless.

Josh is married to his gorgeous wife, Katie, and they have three young children, Lyla, Brody, and Griffin. In his free time, he enjoys reading, traveling, volunteering on several boards in the community, and snowboarding. Connect with Josh any time at joshuaburnette.com.

Pete Hardesty lives in the Washington, D.C. area and serves as the Young Life college divisional coordinator in the Eastern Division. Pete grew up in Baltimore, Maryland, and graduated from the University of Virginia, where he was pre-med with the emphasis on "pre." He then joined the staff of Young Life in Virginia Beach, where he served for seven years before moving to the friendly city of Harrisonburg in 2004.

After being the area director for Young Life in Harrisonburg for eight years, Pete transitioned to start Young Life College at James Madison University in 2012. Pete loves being around college students even though they make him feel old. He crammed his three years of grad school into seventeen and finally received his Master of Divinity from Reformed Theological Seminary in 2014.

A passion for the Middle East has inspired Pete to lead Holy Land trips for the last ten years, with a focus on serving Palestinian kids in the West Bank. He is a frequent international keynote speaker with experience in places such as Asia, Africa, the Middle East, the Caribbean, and all over the US. He is a speaker coach with SCORRE workshops and loves helping people become excellent communicators.

Pete has been working with young people for twenty-five years. They are still his favorite. He loves people and creating environments where they can thrive and achieve their potential. His two nieces are the apple of his eye. Connect with Pete or invite him to speak at PeteHardesty. com and read more of his work at NoRedos.com.

ENDNOTES

1   Antonio Marco Martínez, "Know thyself (Know Yourself)," Antiquitatem, February 26, 2013. http://en.antiquitatem.com/know-thyself-socrates-plato-philosophy.

2   Editorial Staff, "How Much Gold Is Found in the Human Body?," Facts List, April 12, 2016, https://www.factslist.net.

3   "Self-awareness," Lexico Dictionaries, accessed October 26, 2020. https://www.lexico.com/en/definition/self-awareness.

4   Neil Blumenthal, "Why Knowing Yourself Is the Most Important Thing You Can Do," *Inc.*, July 28, 2016, https://www.inc.com/linkedin/neil-blumenthal/know-yourself-neil-blumenthal.html.

5   Jenny Straiton, "Not-So Identical Twins," BioTechniques, November 26, 2018, https://www.biotechniques.com/omics/not-so-identical-twins/.

6   "Links between Childhood Religious Upbringing and Current Religious Identity," Pew Research Center, October 26, 2016, https://www.pewforum.org/2016/10/26/links-between-childhood-religious-upbringing-and-current-religious-identity/.

7   Mark Altaweel, "Geography of Beliefs," Geography Realm, March 4, 2020, https://www.geographyrealm.com/geography-of-beliefs/.

8   Amy Morin, "3 Ways Your Childhood Played a Role in Your Success as an Adult," *Inc.*, August 16, 2017, https://www.inc.com/amy-morin/3-ways-your-childhood-played-a-role-in-your-succes.html.

9   K. Lee Raby et al., "The Enduring Predictive Significance of Early Maternal Sensitivity: Social and Academic Competence Through Age 32 Years," Society for Research in Child Development (John Wiley & Sons, Ltd, December 17, 2014), https://srcd.onlinelibrary.wiley.com/doi/abs/10.1111/cdev.12325.

10   Melia Robinson, "Tim Ferriss: 'You Are the Average of the Five People You Most
      Associate with,'" *Business Insider* (Insider Inc., January 11, 2017), https://www.
      businessinsider.com/tim-ferriss-average-of-five-people-2017-1.

11   David John Seel, *The New Copernicans: Millennials and the Survival of the Church*
      (Nashville, TN: Thomas Nelson, 2018), 145.

12   Robert E, Quinn, *Deep Change: Discovering the Leader Within*, (San Francisco, CA:
      Jossey-Bass, 1996), 176.

13   Nancy J. Adler, "Want to Be an Outstanding Leader? Keep a Journal.," Harvard
      Business Review (Harvard Business Publishing, January 13, 2016), https://hbr.
      org/2016/01/want-to-be-an-outstanding-leader-keep-a-journal.

14   There are many free Enneagram tests online. Here is a sampling: https://www.truity.
      com/test/enneagram-personality-test, https://enneagramacademy.com/enneagram-
      test/.

15   I can recommend five excellent books about habits and growth: *The Power of Habit*
      by Charles Duhigg, *Atomic Habits* by James Clear, *Mindset* by Carol Dweck, *Peak*
      by K. Anders Ericsson and Robert Pool, and *Peak Performance* by Brad Stuhlberg
      and Steve Magness.

16   Brad Stulberg and Steve Magness, *Peak Performance* (PA: Rodale Books, 2017), 55.

17   Nancy Ann Jeffrey, "Sleep Is the New Status Symbol for Successful Entrepreneurs,"
      The Wall Street Journal (Dow Jones & Company, April 2, 1999), http://online.wsj.
      com/article/SB923008887262090895.html.

18   William McRaven, "If You Want to Change the World, Start Off by Making Your
      Bed," Goalcast, August 17, 2017, YouTube video, https://www.youtube.com/
      watch?v=3sK3wJAxGfs.

19 Kerri Anne Kerenzulli, "Completing This Task First Thing in the Morning Takes Seconds—and It Can Make You More Productive All Day," CNBC, March 19, 2019, https://www.cnbc.com/2019/03/18/making-your-bed-first-thing-can-make-you-more-productive-all-day.html.

20 Jon Gordon, Twitter, September 28, 2020.

21 Joel Delgado, "4 Ways to Fail Well," *Relevant* (Relevant Media Group Inc., April 17, 2015), https://relevantmagazine.com.

22 Joseph Luciani, "Why 80 Percent of New Year's Resolutions Fail," *U.S. News & World Report Health*, U.S. News & World Report, December 29, 2015, https://health.usnews.com/health-news/blogs/eat-run/articles/2015-12-29/why-80-percent-of-new-years-resolutions-fail.

23 Jenny Weller, "10 Gym Membership Statistics You Need to Know," Glofox, November 11, 2019, https://www.glofox.com/blog/10-gym-membership-statistics-you-need-to-know/.

24 Angela Duckworth, *Grit: The Power of Passion and Perseverance* (New York: Scribner, 2016), 58.

25 Ibid, 147.

26 Andy Stanley, *Max Q Student Journal*, (New York: Simon & Schuster, 2004), 102.

27 John Rampton, "10 Reasons Why a Mentor Is a Must," *Inc.*, January 9, 2016, https://www.inc.com/john-rampton/10-reasons-why-a-mentor-is-a-must.html.

28 M. Beard, "What Is the Difference between Emotional Intelligence and Emotional Maturity?," Inspire Business Solutions, March 2, 2012, http://inspirebusinesssolutions.com/blog/what-is-the-difference-between-emotional-intelligence-and-emotional-maturity.

29   "Emotional-maturity definitions," Your Dictionary, accessed October 28, 2020, https://www.yourdictionary.com/emotional-maturity.

30   Harvard Business Review, *HBR Guide to Emotional Intelligence (HBR Guide Series)* (Boston: Harvard Business Review Press, 2017), 12.

31   Daniel Goleman, Richard E. Boyatzis, and Annie McKee, *Primal Leadership: Unleashing the Power of Emotional Intelligence* (Boston: Harvard Business Press, 2013), 39.

32   Stephen Covey, quoted in *The Emotional Intelligence Quick Book* by Travis Bradberry and Jean Greaves (New York: Touchstone, 2005), jacket.

33   "New Study: Students Who Can Manages Emotions Do Better Academically and in Life," Growing Leaders, March 10, 2020, https://growingleaders.com/blog/new-study-students-who-can-manage-emotions-do-better-academically-and-in-life/.

34   Carolyn MacCann et al., "Emotional Intelligence Predicts Academic Performance: A Meta-Analysis," *Psychological Bulletin* 146, no. 2 (2020), https://www.apa.org/pubs/journals/releases/bul-bul0000219.pdf.

35   "30 Year Study Reveals the Strongest Predictor of Financial Success," RocheMartin (Rochemartin, 2017), https://www.rochemartin.com/blog/emotional-intelligence-mindfulness-leadership-latest-insights-dan-goleman-eq-summit-2017/.

36   Faye Flam, "Personality Has Greater Impact on Success than IQ, New Research Suggests," *Independent*, August 7, 2017, https://www.independent.co.uk/news/science/personality-iq-success-wealth-factors-determining-prospects-intelligence-careers-james-heckman-a7880376.html.

37   Shawn Andrews, "The Business Case for Emotional Intelligence," workforce.com, September 18, 2018.

38   Travis Bradberry and Jean Greaves, *The Emotional Intelligence Quick Book* (New York: Atria Publishing Group, 2006.), 77.

39   Michael Cornwall, *Go Suck a Lemon: Strategies for Improving Your Emotional Intelligence* (United States: Lulu Enterprises Incorporated, 2010), 177.

40   Ibid., 22.

41   Bradberry and Greaves, *The Emotional Intelligence Quick Book*, 101.

42   Robin Dreeke, *It's Not All About "Me": The Top Ten Techniques for Building Quick Rapport with Anyone* (United States: People Formula, 2011).

43   Bryan Robinson, "The Power of Gratitude and How It Raises Your Happiness Level," *Forbes*, November 18, 2019, https://www.forbes.com/sites/bryanrobinson/2019/11/18/the-power-of-gratitude-and-how-it-raises-your-happiness-level/#5b06f1a373e7.

44   *All the Money in the World*, directed by Ridley Scott (2017; Culver City, CA: Sony Pictures Entertainment Motion Picture Group).

45   "Getty Oil," Wikipedia (Wikimedia Foundation, September 27, 2020), https://en.wikipedia.org/wiki/Getty_Oil.

46   Cornwall, *Go Suck a Lemon,* 53.

47   Justin Bariso, "13 Signs of High Emotional Intelligence," *Inc.*, February 28, 2018, https://www.inc.com/justin-bariso/13-things-emotionally-intelligent-people-do.html.

48   Donna Hatasaki , "Introduction to The Good Way" (presentation, YoungLife, Atlanta, GA, February 11, 2020).

49   Bradberry and Greaves, *The Emotional Intelligence Quick Book,* 39.

50   Kris Gage, "15 Signs of Emotional Maturity," Medium, October 13, 2018, https://medium.com/@krisgage/15-signs-of-emotional-maturity-38b1a2ab9766.

51   Sherrie Campbell, "9 Practices for Achieving Emotional Maturity," *Entrepreneur*, September 22, 2016, https://www.entrepreneur.com/article/282654.

52   "The Importance of Cultural Intelligence within a Global Organization." Randstad, June 8, 2020. https://www.randstad.com/workforce-insights/talent-management/importance-cultural-intelligence-within-a-global-organization/.

53   Kevin Kruse, "What Is Leadership?," *Forbes*, April 9, 2013, https://www.forbes.com/sites/kevinkruse/2013/04/09/what-is-leadership/#2be81ea95b90.

54   Michael Hyatt, "7 Suggestions for Asking More Powerful Questions," Michael Hyatt & Co. (website), August 3, 2016, https://michaelhyatt.com/asking-more-powerful-questions/.

55   Peter Tufano, "'Decent' Leadership: An Old-Fashioned Concept That Is Right for Our Times," Edleman (website), July 27, 2017, https://www.edelman.co.uk/insights/decent-leadership-old-fashioned-concept-right-our-times.

56   Ibid.

57   Bill Boulding, "For Leaders, Decency Is Just as Important as Intelligence," *Harvard Business Review*, July 16, 2019, https://hbr.org/2019/07/for-leaders-decency-is-just-as-important-as-intelligence.

58   "How to Promote Decency in Any Organisation," *Encouraging Appropriate Behaviour* (blog), Savi Consulting Ltd., October 2, 2013, http://www.encouraging-appropriate-behaviour.com/blog/index_files/How-to-promote-decency-in-organisations.php.

59   Nicholas Carr, "The Web Shatters Focus, Rewires Brains," *Wired*, May 24, 2010, https://www.wired.com/2010/05/ff-nicholas-carr/.

60   "How Much Screen Time Is Too Much," Scripps, February 22, 2019, https://www.scripps.org/news_items/6626-how-much-screen-time-is-too-much.

61   Carr, "The Web Shatters Focus."

62   Nicholas Carr, *The Shallows: What the Internet Is Doing to Our Brains* (New York: WW Norton & Company, 2010), 212.

63   Jean M. Twenge and W. Keith Campbell, "Associations Between Screen Time and Lower Psychological Well-Being among Children and Adolescents," National Institutes of Health, December 2018, https://www.ncbi.nlm.nih.gov/pmc/articles/PMC6214874/.

64   Howard LeWine, "Distracted Eating May Add to Weight Gain," Harvard Health Publishing March 29, 2013, https://www.health.harvard.edu/blog/distracted-eating-may-add-to-weight-gain-201303296037.

65   Travis Bradberry "5 Tips for Emotionally Intelligent Emailing," Global Leadership Network July 27, 2017, https://globalleadership.org/articles/leading-yourself/5-tips-emotionally-intelligent-emailing-dr-travis-bradberry/.

66   Ibid.

67   Justin Talbot-Zorn and Leigh Marz, "The Busier You Are, the More You Need Quiet Time," Harvard Business Review, March 17, 2017, https://hbr.org/2017/03/the-busier-you-are-the-more-you-need-quiet-time?utm_source=facebook&utm_campaign=hbr&utm_medium=social.

68   "Meditation: A Simple, Fast Way to Reduce Stress," Mayo Clinic, April 22, 2020, https://www.mayoclinic.org/tests-procedures/meditation/in-depth/meditation/art-20045858.

69   Timothy Ferriss, *Tools of Titans* (New York: Houghton Mifflin Harcourt, 2016).

70   Andrew Hutchinson, "People Are Spending 20% More Time in Apps During the COVID-19 Lockdowns," Social Media Today, April 3, 2020, https://www.socialmediatoday.com/news/people-are-spending-20-more-time-in-apps-during-the-covid-19-lockdowns-re/575403/.

71   Alexandra Samet, "2020 US Social Media Usage: How the Coronavirus Is Changing Consumer Behavior," *Business Insider*, June 9, 2020, https://www.businessinsider.com/2020-us-social-media-usage-report.

72   Ruth Haley Barton, *Invitation to Solitude and Silence* (Downers Grove, IL: InterVarsity Press, 2010), 145.

73   Tish Harrison Warren, *Liturgy of the Ordinary* (Downers Grove, IL: InterVarsity Press, 2016), 143.

74   Clarissa Silva, "Social Media's Impact on Relationships and Self-Esteem," Thrive Global, February 6, 2018, https://thriveglobal.com/stories/social-media-s-impact-on-self-esteem/.

75   Joel Hilchey, "How Many Friends Can 1 Person Have?" (blog), Joel Hilchey (website), October 16, 2017, https://joelhilchey.com/how-many-friends-can-1-person-have/.

76   Lindsay Holmes, "Science Says You Can Really Only Have 5 Close Friends at a Time," *The Huffington Post*, May 4. 2016, https://www.huffpost.com/entry/dunbar-layers-friendship-study_n_5728d4c5e4b016f37893ac14.

77   "Social Media Makes Us Feel Jealous, Ugly and Lonely Say Scientists," The Huffington Post UK, July 25, 2014, https://www.huffingtonpost.co.uk/2014/07/25/social-media-mental-healt_n_5619728.html?ir=UK+Tech&guccounter=1.

78   Leah Fessler, "Scientists Figured Out Why Your Selfies Are Funny and Authentic but Everyone Else's Are So Nacissistic," Quartz, February 17, 2017, https://qz.com/912562/scientists-figured-out-why-your-selfies-are-funny-and-authentic-but-everyone-elses-are-so-narcissistic/.

79   Doug Criss, "More than 250 People around the World Have Died Taking Selfies Since 2011," CNN Health, October 3, 2018, https://www.cnn.com/2018/10/03/health/selfie-deaths-trnd/index.html.

80   "Five Steps to Help Students Avoid the Comparison Trap," Growing Leaders, February 18, 2020, https://growingleaders.com/blog/five-steps-to-help-students-avoid-the-comparison-trap/.

81   Eames Yates, "Here's Why Steve Jobs Never Let His Kids Use an iPad," *Business Insider*, March 4, 2017, https://www.businessinsider.com/heres-why-steve-jobs-never-let-his-kids-use-ipad-apple-social-media-2017-3.

82   Olivia Rudgard, "The Tech Moguls Who Invented Social Media Have Banned Their Children from It," Independent.ie, November 6, 2018, https://www.independent.ie/life/family/parenting/the-tech-moguls-who-invented-social-media-have-banned-their-children-from-it-37494367.html.

83   Warren, *Liturgy of the Ordinary,* 143.

84   Coach Tony, "How to Configure Your iPhone to Work for You, Not Against You," Medium, October 15, 2018, https://medium.com/better-humans/how-to-set-up-your-iphone-for-productivity-focus-and-your-own-longevity-bb27a68cc3d8.

85   M. Szmigiera, "Personal Saving Rate in the U.S. 1960–2019," Statista, February 17, 2020, https://www.statista.com/statistics/246234/personal-savings-rate-in-the-united-states/.

86   Shahram Heshmat, "10 Reasons We Rush for Immediate Gratification," *Psychology Today*, June 6, 2016, https://www.psychologytoday.com/us/blog/science-choice/201606/10-reasons-we-rush-immediate-gratification.

87   Carla Fried, "A self-imposed quest for a perfect time to enjoy an indulgence often means missing out on actually having a good experience," UCLA Anderson Review, January 23, 2019, https://www.anderson.ucla.edu/faculty-and-research/anderson-review/occasion-matching.

88   Alexandra Samuel, "What's So Bad about Instant Gratification?," JSTOR Daily, February 7, 2017, https://daily.jstor.org/whats-bad-instant-gratification/.

89   Barton, *Invitation to Solitude and Silence*, 12.

90   Nir Eyal, *Indistractable* (Dallas: BenBella Books, Inc., 2019), 56.

91   Carr, "The Web Shatters Focus."

92   Maura Thomas, "To Control Your Life, Control What You Pay Attention To," Harvard Business Review, March 15, 2018, https://hbr.org/2018/03/to-control-your-life-control-what-you-pay-attention-to.

93   Vozza, Stephanie. "8 Ways To Improve Your Focus." Fast Company. Fast Company, August 26, 2015. https://www.fastcompany.com/3050123/8-ways-to-improve-your-focus.

94   Adam Grant, "Productivity Isn't about Time Management. It's about Attention Management.," *The New York Times*, March 28, 2019, https://www.nytimes.com/2019/03/28/smarter-living/productivity-isnt-about-time-management-its-about-attention-management.html.

95   Jory MacKay, "When to Work: How to Optimize Your Daily Schedule for Energy, Motivation, and Focus," RescueTime (blog), September 11, 2018, https://blog.rescuetime.com/when-to-work-productivity-curves/.

96   Justin Talbot-Zorn and Leigh Marz, "The Busier You Are, the More You Need Quiet Time," Harvard Business Review, March 17, 2017, https://hbr.org/2017/03/the-busier-you-are-the-more-you-need-quiet-time?utm_source=facebook&utm_campaign=hbr&utm_medium=social.

97   Thomas William Jackson, Ray Dawson, and Darren Wilson, "Understanding Email Interaction Increases Organizational Productivity," ResearchGate, August 2003, https://www.researchgate.net/publication/28575079_Understanding_email_interaction_increases_organizational_productivity.

98   Jory Mackay, "Communication Overload: Our Research Shows Most Workers Can't Go 6 Minutes Without Checking Email or IM," RescueTime (blog), July 11, 2018, https://blog.rescuetime.com/communication-multitasking-switches/.

99   Jory MacKay, "How to Focus: The 5 Key Elements for Attention Management, Focus, and Flow," RescueTime (blog), October 30, 2018, https://blog.rescuetime.com/finding-focus/.

100 Nir Eyal, Indistractable, 156.

101 Adam Green, "A Pickpocket's Tale: The Spectacular Thefts of Apollo Robbins," The New Yorker, January 7, 2013.

102 Luna Greenstein, "The Difference Between a Disorder and a Feeling," National Alliance on Mental Illness, October, 10, 2019, https://www.nami.org/Blogs/NAMI-Blog/October-2019/The-Difference-Between-a-Disorder-and-a-Feeling.

103 Benoit Denizet-Lewis, "Why Are More American Teenagers Than Ever Suffering From Severe Anxiety?," The New York Times Magazine, October 11, 2017, https://www.nytimes.com/2017/10/11/magazine/why-are-more-american-teenagers-than-ever-suffering-from-severe-anxiety.html.

104 Nicole J. LeBlanc and Luana Marques, "Anxiety in College: What We Know and How to Cope," Harvard Health Publishing, August 27, 2019, https://www.health.harvard.edu/blog/anxiety-in-college-what-we-know-and-how-to-cope-2019052816729.

105 Emily Tate, "Anxiety on the Rise," *Inside Higher Ed*, March 29, 2017, https://www.insidehighered.com/news/2017/03/29/anxiety-and-depression-are-primary-concerns-students-seeking-counseling-services.

106 Center for Collegiate Mental Health. (2020, January). 2019 Annual Report (Publication No. STA 20-244).

107 "Any Anxiety Disorder," National Institute of Mental Health, November 2017, https://www.nimh.nih.gov/health/statistics/any-anxiety-disorder.shtml.

108 "Facts & Statistics," Anxiety and Depression Association of America, accessed October 31, 2020, https://adaa.org/about-adaa/press-room/facts-statistics.

109 Neighborhood Psychiatry, "Why 75 Percent of Anxiety Sufferers Fail to Get Proper Care," *Psychology Today*, August 13, 2018, https://www.psychologytoday.com/us/blog/psychiatry-the-people/201808/why-75-percent-anxiety-sufferers-fail-get-proper-care.

110 "The Difference between Regular Feelings of Anxiety and a True Anxiety Disorder," *ULifeline*, The JED Foundation, accessed October 31, 2020, http://www.ulifeline.org/articles/439-anxiety-vs-anxiety-disorders.

111 "Anxiety," American Psychological Association, accessed October 31, 2020, https://www.apa.org/topics/anxiety/.

112 Adam Felman, "What to Know about Anxiety," *Medical News Today*, Healthline Media UK Ltd., January 11, 2020, https://www.medicalnewstoday.com/articles/323454.

113 Luna Greenstein, "The Difference Between a Disorder and a Feeling," National
     Alliance on Mental Illness, October, 10, 2019, https://www.nami.org/Blogs/NAMI-
     Blog/October-2019/The-Difference-Between-a-Disorder-and-a-Feeling.

114 Scott Stossel, *My Age of Anxiety* (New York: Alfred A. Knopf, 2014), 14.

115 "10 Reasons Teens Have So Much Anxiety Today," *Psychology Today*, November 3,
     2017, https://www.psychologytoday.com/us/blog/what-mentally-strong-people-
     dont-do/201711/10-reasons-teens-have-so-much-anxiety-today?fbclid=IwAR2LsR
     nU0qDFUU0H7oNPmA8REfCos0tL6PWtxNGfc8rXoR1qTRseRcAULYE

116 Jean M. Twenge, Gabrielle N. Martin, and W. Keith Campbell, "Decreases in
     psychological well-being among American adolescents after 2012 and links
     to screen time during the rise of smartphone technology," National Library of
     Medicine, September 2018, https://www.ncbi.nlm.nih.gov/pubmed/29355336.

117 Joel Brown, "Anxiety and Depression," BU Today, October 2, 2016, http://www.
     bu.edu/articles/2016/college-students-anxiety-and-depression.

118 Melinda Smith, Lawrence Robinson, and Jeanne Segal, "Anxiety Disorders and
     Anxiety Attacks," HelpGuide, September 2020, https://www.helpguide.org/articles/
     anxiety/anxiety-disorders-and-anxiety-attacks.htm.

119 Joel Brown, "Anxiety and Depression," BU Today, October 2, 2016, http://www.
     bu.edu/articles/2016/college-students-anxiety-and-depression.

120 AnnaVannuccia, Kaitlin M. Flannery, and Christine McCauley Ohannessian,
     "Social Media Use and Anxiety in Emerging Adults," *Journal of Affective Disorders*
     207, (January 2017): 163–166, https://www.sciencedirect.com/science/article/abs/
     pii/S0165032716309442.

121 Matthew Sloan, "Ease Anxiety and Stress: Take a (Belly) Breather," Harvard Health
     Publishing, April 26, 2019, https://www.health.harvard.edu/blog/ease-anxiety-and-
     stress-take-a-belly-breather-2019042616521.

122   Melinda Smith, Robert Segal, and Jeanne Segal, "Therapy for Anxiety Disorders," HelpGuide, September 2020, https://www.helpguide.org/articles/anxiety/therapy-for-anxiety-disorders.htm.

123   Dr. Tim. Elmore, *Generation Z Unfiltered* (United States: Poet Gardener Publishing, 2019), 152.

124   Nicole J. LeBlanc and Luana Marques, "Anxiety in College: What We Know and How to Cope," Harvard Health Publishing, August 27, 2019, https://www.health.harvard.edu/blog/anxiety-in-college-what-we-know-and-how-to-cope-2019052816729.

125   "The Five Greatest Predictors of Student Success" (blog), Growing Leaders, January 11, 2013, https://growingleaders.com/blog/student-success/.

126   Luna Greenstein, "The Difference Between a Disorder and a Feeling," National Alliance on Mental Illness, October, 10, 2019, https://www.nami.org/Blogs/NAMI-Blog/October-2019/The-Difference-Between-a-Disorder-and-a-Feeling.

127   Ibid.

128   "What Is Depression?," American Psychiatric Association, October 2020, https://www.psychiatry.org/patients-families/depression/what-is-depression.

129   Karyn Hede, "Destigmatizing Depression," *Science*, October 2, 2009, https://www.sciencemag.org/careers/2009/10/destigmatizing-depression.

130   "Quotes About Depression & What Depression Feels Like," *Psycom*, Remedy Health Media, last modified September 3, 2020, https://www.psycom.net/depression-what-depression-feels-like.

131   "Depression Often Stress in Childhood," WebMD, accessed October 31, 2020, https://www.webmd.com/depression/features/depression-often-starts-in-childhood#1.

132 "Major Depression," National Institute of Mental Health, February 2019, https://www.nimh.nih.gov/health/statistics/major-depression.shtml.

133 "Depression in Women: Understanding the Gender Gap," Mayo Clinic, January 29, 2019, https://www.mayoclinic.org/diseases-conditions/depression/in-depth/depression/art-20047725.

134 "Depression Statistics," Depression and Bipolar Support Alliance, accessed October 31, 2020, https://www.dbsalliance.org/education/depression/statistics/.

135 Susan Scutti, "Michael Phelps: 'I Am Extremely Thankful That I Did Not Take My Life,'" CNN, January 20, 2018, https://www.cnn.com/2018/01/19/health/michael-phelps-depression/index.html.

136 "Types of Depression," WebMD, accessed October 31, 2020, https://www.webmd.com/depression/guide/depression-types.

137 "Causes of Depression," WebMD, accessed October 31, 2020, https://www.webmd.com/depression/guide/causes-depression#1.

138 A. Brownawell and K. Kelley, "Psychotherapy Is Effective and Here's Why," *Monitor on Psychology* 42, No. 9 (October 2011): 14, https://www.apa.org/monitor/2011/10/psychotherapy.

139 Ellen Driessen and Steven D. Hollon, "Cognitive Behavioral Therapy for Mood Disorders: Efficacy, Moderators and Mediators," *The Psychiatric Clinics of North America* 33, no. 3 (September 2011): 537–555, https://www.ncbi.nlm.nih.gov/pmc/articles/PMC2933381/.

140 "Overcoming Depression: How Psychologists Help with Depressive Disorders," American Psychological Association, October 1, 2016, https://www.apa.org/helpcenter/depression.

141 "Interpersonal Psychotherapy," *Psychology Today*, accessed October 31, 2020, https://www.psychologytoday.com/us/therapy-types/interpersonal-psychotherapy.

142 "Depression," National Institute of Mental Health, February 2018, https://www.nimh.nih.gov/health/topics/depression/index.shtml.

143 Crystal Raypole, "How to Help a Depressed Friend," Healthline, May 29, 2019, https://www.healthline.com/health/how-to-help-a-depressed-friend.

144 Melinda Smith, Lawrence Robinson, and Jeanne Segal, "Helping Someone with Depression," HelpGuide, September 2020, https://www.helpguide.org/articles/depression/helping-someone-with-depression.htm.

145 "7 Great Reasons Why You Should Move to Austin, Texas," Austin Relocation Guide, accessed November 1, 2020, http://www.austinrelocationguide.com/7-Great-Reasons-Why-You-Should-Move-To-Austin-Texas/.

146 Sharon Jayson, "Millennials, Generation Z: Connected with thousands of friends – but feeling all alone," USA Today, March 7, 2019, https://www.usatoday.com/story/news/health/2019/03/07/millennial-generation-z-social-media-connected-loneliness-cigna-health-study/3090013002/.

147 Jayne O'Donnell and Shari Rudavsky, "Young Americans are the loneliest, surprising study from Cigna shows," USA Today, May 1, 2018, https://www.usatoday.com/story/news/politics/2018/05/01/loneliness-poor-health-reported-far-more-among-young-people-than-even-those-over-72/559961002/.

148 "These Three Moves Will Help You Stop Feeling Lonely," Psychology Today, December 11, 2017, https://www.psychologytoday.com/us/blog/brainstorm/201712/these-three-moves-will-help-you-stop-feeling-lonely.

149 "Lonely," Dictionary.com, accessed November 1, 2020, https://www.dictionary.com/browse/loneliness.

150   Julianne Holt-Lunstad ,Timothy B. Smith, and J. Bradley Layton, "Social
      Relationships and Mortality Risk: A Meta-analytic Review," PLOS Medicine,
      July 27, 2010, https://journals.plos.org/plosmedicine/article?id=10.1371/journal.
      pmed.1000316.

151   Jefferson M. Fish, "Guilt and Shame," Psychology Today, September 20, 2016,
      https://www.psychologytoday.com/us/blog/looking-in-the-cultural-mirror/201609/
      guilt-and-shame.

152   Lindsay Dodgson, "A Psychotherapist Says There Are 4 Types of Shame—Here's
      What They Are and How They Affect Us," Business Insider, April 3, 2018, https://
      www.businessinsider.com/different-types-of-shame-2018-3.

153   David Sack, "5 Ways to Silence Shame," Psychology Today, January 13, 2015, https://
      www.psychologytoday.com/us/blog/where-science-meets-the-steps/201501/5-
      ways-silence-shame.

154   Rebecca Webber, "The Comparison Trap," Psychology Today, November 7, 2017,
      https://www.psychologytoday.com/us/articles/201711/the-comparison-trap.

155   Liz Mineo, "Good Genes Are Nice, but Joy Is Better," The Harvard Gazette, April
      22, 2017, https://news.harvard.edu/gazette/story/2017/04/over-nearly-80-years-
      harvard-study-has-been-showing-how-to-live-a-healthy-and-happy-life/.

156   Robert Waldinger, "What Makes a Good Life? Lessons from the Longest Study on
      Happiness," TEDxBeaconStreet, accessed November 1, 2020, https://www.ted.com/
      talks/robert_waldinger_what_makes_a_good_life_lessons_from_the_longest_
      study_on_happiness.

157   "Caring for Someone Who's Lonely," Age UK, August 19, 2020, https://www.ageuk.
      org.uk/information-advice/health-wellbeing/loneliness/caring-for-someone-whos-
      lonely/.

158 Henry Nouwen, *Who Are We?*, read by Henry Nouwen (Rockville: Learn 25, 2017), Audible audio, 59 min.

159 David G. Benner, *The Gift of Being Yourself* (Downers Grove, IL: InterVarsity Press, 2004): 83. I am deeply indebted to David Benner and his magnificent book for several insights in this chapter and for my personal spiritual journey.

160 Ibid., 22.

161 Ibid., 47.

162 Ibid., 83.

163 David G. Benner, *Surrender to Love* (Downers Grove, IL: InterVarsity Press, 2003): 16.

164 Barton, *Invitation to Solitude and Silence*, 116–117.